# GHOSTS ON
# THE SOMME

# GHOSTS ON THE SOMME

## Filming the Battle, June–July 1916

*Alastair H. Fraser, Andrew Robertshaw and Steve Roberts*

Foreword by Roger Smither

Maps by Keith Maddison

Pen & Sword
**MILITARY**

First published in Great Britain in 2009 by
Pen & Sword Military
an imprint of
Pen & Sword Books Ltd
47 Church Street
Barnsley
South Yorkshire
S70 2AS

ISBN 978 1 4415 836 2

Typeset in Ehrhardt by
Phoenix Typesetting, Auldgirth, Dumfriesshire

Printed and bound in England by
CPI UK

Pen & Sword Books Ltd incorporates the Imprints of Pen & Sword Aviation,
Pen & Sword Maritime, Pen & Sword Military, Wharncliffe Books,
Pen & Sword Select, Pen & Sword Military Classics and Leo Cooper.

For a complete list of Pen & Sword titles please contact
PEN & SWORD BOOKS LIMITED
47 Church Street, Barnsley, South Yorkshire, S70 2AS, England
E-mail: enquiries@pen-and-sword.co.uk
Website: www.pen-and-sword.co.uk

# CONTENTS

The Publishers have included several historically important wartime photographs that cannot be reproduced to our usual high standards. It was felt that they were of sufficient interest to the reader to be included.

# ABBREVIATIONS

| | |
|---|---|
| ADD | Accumulated Degree Days (Forensic) |
| ADS | Advanced Dressing Station |
| CCS | Casualty Clearing Station |
| CMG | Companion of the Order of St Michael and St George |
| CP | Collecting Post |
| CWGC | Commonwealth War Graves Commission |
| DH | *Sir Douglas Haig's great push* |
| DSO | Distinguished Service Order |
| FOO | Forward Observation Officer |
| GHQ | General Headquarters |
| GS | General Service |
| HTMB | Heavy Trench Mortar Battery |
| IR | Infanterie Regiment (German) |
| IWM | Imperial War Museum |
| KW | *Kinematograph Weekly* |
| MC | Military Cross |
| MDS | Main Dressing Station |
| MGC | Machine Gun Corps |
| NCO | Non-commissioned Officer |
| OH | *History of the Great War based on Official Documents* |
| RAMC | Royal Army Medical Corps |
| RAP | Regimental Aid Post |
| RIR | Reserve Infanterie Regiment (German) |
| RMO | Regimental Medical Officer |
| SAA | Small Arms Ammunition |
| SC | *Screen* |
| TBS | Total Body Score (Forensic) |
| TF | Territorial Force |
| TMB | Trench Mortar Battery |
| VC | Victoria Cross |
| VN | IWM Viewing Notes |

# ACKNOWLEDGEMENTS

This project has involved many people who have helped with photographs, information, time, driving, hospitality and advice; space prevents full explanations but we are extremely grateful to everyone for their assistance, many above and beyond the call of duty.

Family: Minnie, Simon, Freya and Alice Fraser, Kate and Ian Mellor, Ruth Fanshawe; Lesley Wood and Anthony Roberts; Janice and Lilly Robertshaw.

Pen and Sword: Rupert Harding, Sarah Cook and Jon Wilkinson.

Malins family: June Bristow, Lisa Siorvanes.

Imperial War Museum: Toby Haggith, Hilary Roberts, Tom Adams, George Smith and the staff of the Library and Photograph Archive. Special thanks to Roger Smither for the Foreword and much valuable advice.

Yap Films: Pauline Duffy, Elliott Halpern, Herrie Ten Cate, Robert Guerin, Peter Sawade, Mary Petryshyn, and especially Judy Ruyzlo.

London Scottish Regimental Museum: Major Stuart Young and Clem Webb.

No-Man's-Land: all our friends and colleagues, particularly Dave Kenyon, Pete Moore, Dan Phillips, Richard Culyer, Ralph Whitehead, Alexander and Petra Brunotte, and for the maps Keith Maddison.

Fusiliers Museum, Bury: Col. Mike Glover, Tony Sprayson, Paul Dalton, Helen Castle.

Lip-reading: Jessica Rees.

National Media Museum, Bradford: Ruth Kitchin, Michael Harvey.

Oceanvillas Tea Rooms, Auchonvillers: Avril and Mark Williams as always.

Individuals: Kevin Brownlow, Paul Reed, Martin Pegler, Steve Hurst, David Pinney, Professor Alf Linney, Dr Nicholas Hiley, Dr Nicholas Saunders, Dr Tal Simmons, Chris McCarthy, Dr Francis Jones, Paul Blackett and Clive Bowery.

Alastair Fraser
Andrew Robertshaw
Steve Roberts
April 2008

# MAPS

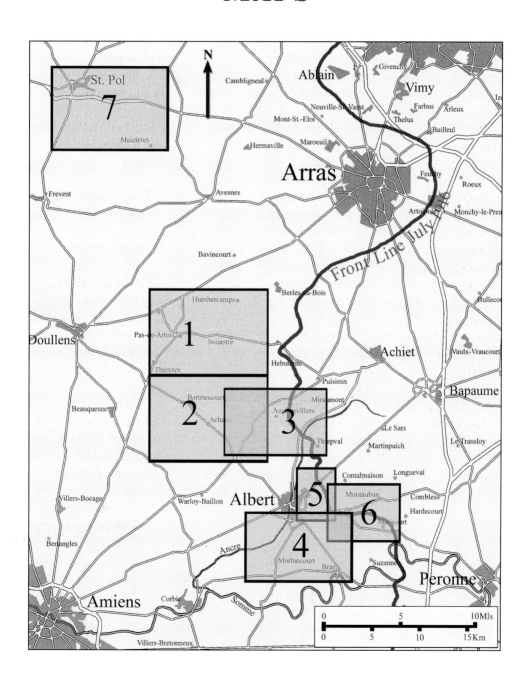

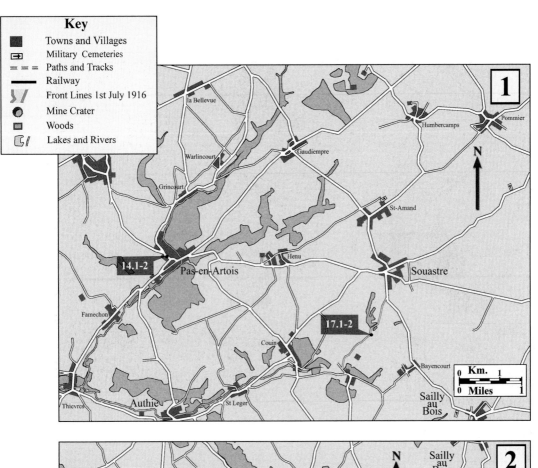

## Key

■ Towns and Villages
⊞ Military Cemeteries
= = = Paths and Tracks
— Railway
⚐ Front Lines 1st July 1916
● Mine Crater
▫ Woods
▨ Lakes and Rivers

**1**

la Bellevue

Humbercamps

Pommier

N

Warlincourt

Gaudiempre

Grincourt

St-Amand

14.1-2

Henu

Pas-en-Artois

Souastre

Famechon

17.1-2

Couin

Bayencourt

Km.

Miles

Thievres

Authie

St Leger

Sailly au Bois

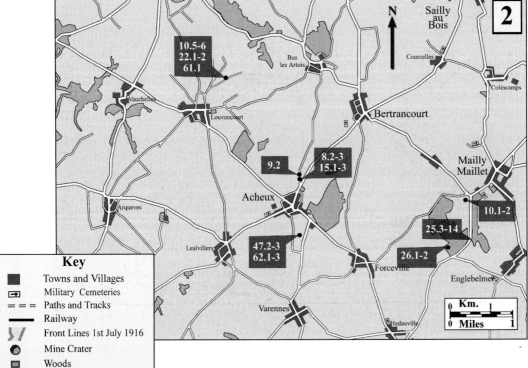

**2**

N

Sailly au Bois

10.5-6
22.1-2
61.1

Bus les Artois

Courcelles

Colincamps

Vauchelles

Louvencourt

Bertrancourt

Mailly Maillet

9.2

8.2-3
15.1-3

Acheux

10.1-2

Arqueves

25.3-14

47.2-3
62.1-3

Lealvillers

26.1-2

Forceville

Englebelmer

Varennes

Km.

Miles

Hedauville

## Key

■ Towns and Villages
⊞ Military Cemeteries
= = = Paths and Tracks
— Railway
⚐ Front Lines 1st July 1916
● Mine Crater
▫ Woods
▨ Lakes and Rivers

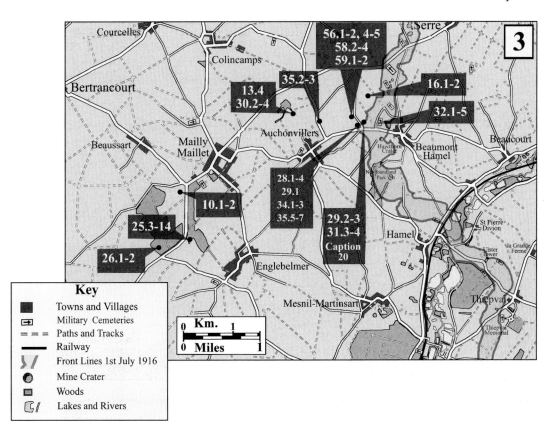

Map 3

- 56.1-2, 4-5
- 58.2-4
- 59.1-2
- Serre
- Courcelles
- Colincamps
- 35.2-3
- 16.1-2
- Bertrancourt
- 13.4
- 30.2-4
- 32.1-5
- Auchonvillers
- Beaucourt
- Hawthorn Crater
- Beaumont Hamel
- Beaussart
- Mailly Maillet
- Newfoundland Park
- 28.1-4
- 29.1
- 34.1-3
- 35.5-7
- 10.1-2
- 29.2-3
- 31.3-4
- Caption 20
- St Pierre Divion
- 25.3-14
- Hamel
- La Grande Ferme
- Ulster Tower
- 26.1-2
- Englebelmer
- Thiepval
- Mesnil-Martinsart
- Thiepval Memorial

**Key**

| | |
|---|---|
| ■ | Towns and Villages |
| ⊟ | Military Cemeteries |
| = = = | Paths and Tracks |
| — | Railway |
| ⟋⟍ | Front Lines 1st July 1916 |
| ● | Mine Crater |
| ▣ | Woods |
| ⟦⟍ | Lakes and Rivers |

0 Km. 1
0 Miles 1

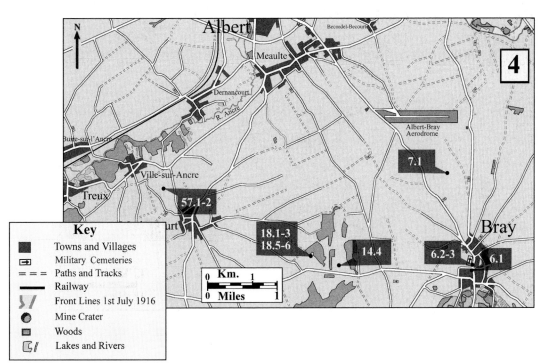

Map 4

- N
- Albert
- Becordel-Becourt
- Meaulte
- 4
- Dernancourt
- R. Ancre
- Albert-Bray Aerodrome
- Buire-sur-l'Ancre
- 7.1
- Ville-sur-Ancre
- Treux
- Bray
- ...urt
- 57.1-2
- 18.1-3
- 18.5-6
- 14.4
- 6.2-3
- 6.1

**Key**

| | |
|---|---|
| ■ | Towns and Villages |
| ⊟ | Military Cemeteries |
| = = = | Paths and Tracks |
| — | Railway |
| ⟋⟍ | Front Lines 1st July 1916 |
| ● | Mine Crater |
| ▣ | Woods |
| ⟦⟍ | Lakes and Rivers |

0 Km. 1
0 Miles 1

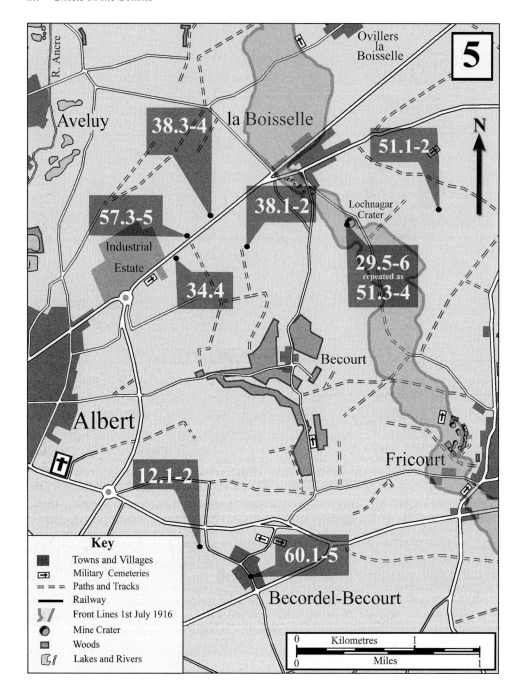

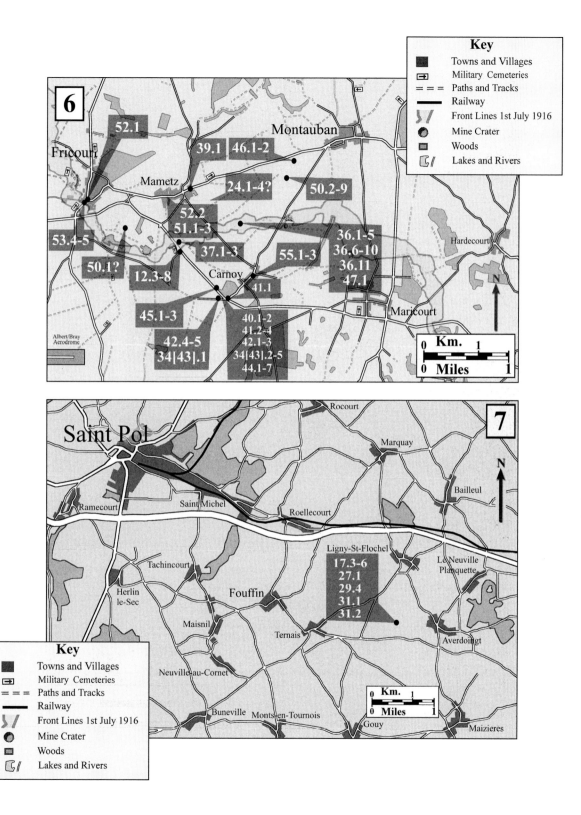

# FOREWORD

*The Battle of the Somme* has long been recognised as one of the jewels in the collection of the Imperial War Museum's Film and Video Archive, an opinion formally endorsed in 2005 when the film became the first item of British documentary heritage to be accepted for inscription on UNESCO's 'Memory of the World' register. To mark this honour, as well as the 90th anniversary of the end of the First World War, the Museum in 2008 published *The Battle of the Somme* on a new DVD, featuring a full digital restoration of the film and two different, specially recorded musical accompaniments.

As the Museum's application for UNESCO registration made plain, *The Battle of the Somme* is important both as the world's first feature-length battlefield document-ary and for a number of other reasons. These include the precedents it set in propaganda technique, the issues it raised about the portrayal of warfare for a general audience, and the role it played in turning film from a little-valued form of mass enter-tainment into a medium worthy of inclusion in the collections of a major national museum.

The film's greatest importance, however, and the reason for its astonishing success with British cinema audiences on its release in 1916, was the feeling among members of those audiences that the film was making it possible for them to share some of the reality of what their husbands, sons, brothers, neighbours and other loved ones were experiencing in the actual battle of the Somme.

This sense of engagement with reality has continued through the years following the end of the First World War. The film is the source of several of the most iconic images used to invoke the Western Front, the First World War or even twentieth-century warfare in general in popular imagination. Images such as the great mine explosion at Beaumont Hamel, the nervous troops in the Sunken Lane, the 'over the top' charge, the 'trench rescue' of a wounded comrade, the treatment of casualties and the faces of the survivors are all very familiar to millions of people who have no idea where they originated.

The fact that one of those images – 'over the top' – is now universally recognised as a scene deliberately staged for the camera rather than a piece of actual combat filming has added another element to the reputation of the film, contributing in some people's minds to a cynical 'understanding' that much war film is heavily tainted by the practice of faking.

The Imperial War Museum has devoted considerable attention to examining the question of the authenticity and thus the historical value of its films. As early as 4 May 1922 the Museum arranged a screening for a panel of Trustees and invited experts to comment in these terms on *The Battle of the Somme* and other titles. This tradition of examination, research and evaluation has continued and been encouraged ever since, not least from a feeling of responsibility towards the cameramen whose work is preserved in the Archive, and whose bravery and integrity are challenged every time a generalised or unfounded accusation of faking is made.

The Museum has never, however, had the time or the resources to pursue the kind of detailed analysis that has been undertaken by Alastair Fraser, Andrew Robertshaw and Steve Roberts for the present book. We first met this team when they were working with YAP Films on a 2006 television programme called *Battle of the Somme – The True Story* and have followed with interest the extraordinary range of material they have uncovered and freely shared with us, as well as the variety of forensic techniques they have used, as they continued their research for *Ghosts on the Somme*.

The fact that *Ghosts* confidently endorses the authenticity of the vast majority of the footage shot by the film's two cameramen, Geoffrey Malins and J.B. McDowell, at the end of June and the start of July 1916 is a gratifying corrective to the kind of glib assumptions mentioned earlier. At the same time, the quantity of evidence produced to justify reinterpretation of so much of the traditional understanding of exactly which units or individuals were filmed, where, on what occasion and by whom, will give everybody who thinks they know the film much food for thought for many years to come. *Ghosts on the Somme* sets a new standard for the examination of archive documentary film and is more than welcome as a result. The availability of this book will greatly enhance the understanding of those who view *The Battle of the Somme* and are interested in the detailed history of what they are watching.

Roger Smither
Keeper, Film and Photograph Archives
Imperial War Museum

CHAPTER ONE

# INTRODUCTION AND METHODOLOGY

*The Battle of the Somme* has attracted tremendous attention since its release in August 1916. It had a profound effect upon contemporary cinema-goers and continues to move and inform the audience of the early twenty-first century. There is now nobody alive who took part in those terrible battles of 1916 and the film very much takes their place in the modern imagination of what the Great War was like. The scholarly comment on the film looks at it as media history and asks what the film meant to those watching it in 1916 and whether it was effective propaganda. One aspect of the film has been neglected, however: what are we actually looking at? Who are these men and where are they? What are they doing and when? The viewing notes produced by the Imperial War Museum team represent the only attempt to look at the film from this viewpoint and we acknowledge our gratitude to the authors. We believe that we have built upon their work and taken our understanding of the film considerably further.

As military historians, we examine the film to determine its value as an historical document. We have many years of experience in researching the Great War and as members of No-Man's-Land, the European Group for Great War Archaeology which has been excavating and recording sites along the Western Front since 1997. Great War archaeology is a truly multi-disciplinary endeavour, using documentary sources and the 'hands-on' skills of landscape archaeology, forensic science, aerial photographic interpretation, geophysical survey and field walking. It seemed to us that we might be able to use these skills to unlock other secrets of the Great War that exist on film rather than under the ground.

In the film we can learn a great deal about the British Army in June and July 1916. We see what it looked like, how it was fed, clothed, armed, supplied and went about trying to break the formidable German defences, and how in some areas it succeeded in this task. The images of dead and wounded had a profound effect upon contemporaries and are a moving record of the price of war. The question of whether such scenes should be shown is still a controversial issue in the early twenty-first century. It is clear from fairly accurate estimates that more than half the population of the British Isles saw the film in 1916. No film until *Star Wars* in the 1970s has commanded a comparable audience. In the recent past the most widely seen image is the explosion of the

Hawthorn Ridge mine, shown in virtually every popular documentary on the Great War; few non-specialist viewers have any idea what it is they are seeing. The explosion itself often appears in isolation and without the poorer quality and less spectacular scenes of troops advancing on the crater. Without understanding where and when it was taken it is not apparent that this seemingly unremarkable footage was filmed at considerable risk and shows men dying in action on the bright, sunny morning of one of the most significant days in British history – 1 July 1916.

We have tried to get behind the footage and give it meaning. Each scene has a context in time and space which can be revealed with careful research. Some men seen in the film were killed within hours; some were killed later in the war; others survived to lead productive lives, fight in a second great war, and to have children and grand-children. We know of one man in the film who endured the awful fate of losing a son in the Second World War. By identifying individuals in the film we can tell the story of how they came to be there. Most of the men pictured are nameless, unidentifiable figures but their condition is no less poignant for that. Sometimes the camera gives us fragments of the lives of men who have names and histories. We can tell how they came to be there and what happened to them after the filming stopped. In a few instances we can even report what they were saying while they were being filmed. We also discovered that this can be a two-way process and can help us to deduce where and when some scenes were shot. We can return much footage to the historical record by fixing it as a portrayal of known events at a specific time. Some scenes have eluded detection, as they contain too few clues for identification. We would welcome any information on these shots from readers.

We have gone back to first principles with every scene in the film, re-examining every deduction made by other commentators, looking at each scene in detail and comparing it with other sources:

- The collection of stills held by the Imperial War Museum is an important source for the study of the film. Many of these were taken by Ernest Brooks, who accompanied Geoffrey Malins during filming. They were often taken next to the ciné cameraman and can supply additional information. Indeed, in some instances Malins himself appears in the photograph. However, the captions are often inaccurate and need careful interpretation.
- Malins wrote a book describing his career as a combat photographer up to 1917. This work, entitled *How I filmed the war*, was aimed at the cinema audience and was not particularly well received by his colleagues or the military. Publication was withheld until 1920. The section on the Battle of the Somme is the best source that we have but it must be treated with care. Malins' account is generally accurate where it can be verified but there are major omissions and it is difficult to establish a reliable chronology from it.
- An important and previously unused source is the 'tie-in' book of the film *Sir Douglas Haig's great push: the Battle of the Somme*. Issued initially in 1916 as

a part work, it was also published in book form in 1917. This has numerous screen grabs that do not exist in the IWM collections and also provides important clues to footage no longer extant in the surviving print. The part work edition is available in facsimile from the Naval and Military Press.

- The 'dope sheet' is a list of shots in caption order setting out when, where and by whom each shot was filmed. Compiled between 1918 and 1922, as a near-contemporary document this should provide the final word but it has proved to be highly inaccurate in every respect. It is another source to be treated with caution.

- War diaries from battalion up to army level in the National Archives provide important information on the identity of men and units, and some material about the distribution of the film is to be found in classes FO395 and INF4.

- We have also undertaken a thorough examination of the landscape of the Somme battlefield looking for clues. However, this is a ninety-year-old trail that has gone very cold. McDowell and Brooks left little record and both are long dead.

As we mentioned earlier, the Imperial War Museum's viewing notes to accompany the video release represent the most recent study of the film. Edited by Roger Smither with contributions from many of the museum's experts, they are entitled *The Battle of the Somme* and *The Battle of the Ancre and the Advance of the Tanks*.

The most notorious allegation levelled at the film is that some of it was faked. Close examination confirms that there are degrees of faking present, but the issue is not a simple one; the reasons for faking have more to do with the technical limitations of the equipment than any lack of courage on the part of the operators. Malins was awarded an OBE and McDowell earned an MC later in the war. That no British or Empire cameraman was killed in action was a matter of good luck despite their willingness to put themselves in the way of danger. We can, however, prove that certain scenes, making up a very small proportion of the film, were shot on a training area. Some footage that was previously said to have been shot away from the front line is in fact genuine, while other scenes, although filmed in the front line, are not correctly captioned. We believe that we have set the record straight with regard to this.

We leave the film on the day of the first public showing on 21 August 1916; the reaction to the film, both at home and abroad, is another story and we hope to look at this, together with an analysis of *The King visits his armies*, *The Battle of the Ancre and the Advance of the Tanks* and the German and French films of the Somme in another volume.

The book is not merely a highly detailed set of viewing notes, although it can be used for that purpose by reference to the table of shots in the appendix. We have attempted to set out the movements of both cameramen chronologically, ascribing to them the footage they took in the order in which it was shot, not the order in which it appears in the film. Some scenes have proved impossible to allocate to a specific cameraman and we have sometimes had to make a best guess at the time and place; however, every scene in the film is discussed at some point in the book, even if some have defeated us. The book is not a military history of the Battle of the Somme; units and their deeds are discussed where relevant but the books cited in the bibliography will provide much fuller information. For walking the battlefield we recommend both the Pen & Sword *Battleground Europe* series and the reproduction trench maps produced by G.H. Smith & Son of Easingwold.

Unfortunately some of the comparison photographs in the book are not exact matches. The Somme battlefield is mostly farmland and we feel strongly that we do not have any right to walk into the middle of crops or to trespass on private land to take photographs. We would urge anybody following our work to do the same and respect the rights of landowners. The villages of the Somme battlefield have changed greatly in the last ninety years, making it difficult to locate some of the footage in the film. All modern photographs were taken by the authors unless otherwise stated. Some older photographs are of poor quality but are the best examples that we can obtain. Every effort has been made to trace copyright ownership but this has not proved possible in every case. We apologise for any omissions and will be pleased to credit material appropriately in any future edition.

As archaeologists of the Great War we are acutely aware of the danger of un-exploded munitions which we uncover on a regular basis; we owe a constant debt to our explosive ordnance disposal personnel for keeping us all safe. Munitions from the Great War are not souvenirs – they were designed to kill and are all still potentially deadly in the hands of both expert and non-expert. Only people who have undergone a course in ordnance disposal are experts. **Do not dismantle munitions or take them home with you; the legal penalties are severe and the consequences of an accident could be disastrous to you, your family, friends and fellow travellers.**

## CHAPTER TWO

# THE BACKGROUND TO
# *THE BATTLE OF THE SOMME*

The moving picture show was a relatively new phenomenon in 1914 as the first public performances had begun only in the 1890s. It had become a sophisticated and profitable industry which had quickly established itself as part of working-class culture, even if sections of the middle and upper classes were indifferent or hostile to it. Many cinemas were lavish, purpose-built 'picture palaces'. The programmes were varied and included the newsreel or 'topical' film which showed current events in Britain and around the world. Estimates vary as to the number of cinemas in Britain but there were probably over 4,000, selling perhaps 20,000,000 tickets a week. The assumption in August 1914 was that there would be facilities to film the war as it unfolded, but this was not the case. Army officers, particularly the new Secretary of State for War, Lord Kitchener, had little sympathy for cinema and a fierce prejudice against the press in any form. With exaggerated concerns about security on the part of the War Office and GHQ in France this meant that very little useful or reliable news reached the public. While it was apparent that the British public was almost unanimously supportive of the war, there was concern about Britain's image abroad. The Cabinet approved the formation of a highly secret body known as the Wellington House Committee under the leadership of the Liberal politician Charles Masterman. This was to promote British war aims in neutral countries as well as to counter German propaganda. Much of their output was printed material but the Cinema Committee at Wellington House produced one major film, *Britain prepared*, which was partly shot in colour by Charles Urban. It was first shown in December 1915 and enjoyed reasonable success.[1]

Although initially both journalists and film cameramen were able to operate in the Belgian sector, it became impossible to work without the cooperation of the military authorities. A few war correspondents were allowed to France in May 1915 but attempts to get permission to film on the Western Front were refused by the War Office. The major newsreel companies, Barker, British and Colonial, Éclair, Gaumont, Jury's Imperial Pictures, Kineto and The Topical Film Company formed a body known as the Topical Committee of the Kinematographic Manufacturers' Association. After much negotiation with the War Office, guided by the Committee's secretary Joseph Brooke Wilkinson, an agreement was signed on 25 October 1915.

Two cameramen were supplied by the Committee who found their equipment, expenses and wages. Additionally 'plant, machinery, dark room equipment and staff' were provided by the firms making up the Committee. In return for the exclusive right to film in France the Committee was to handle the distribution of its productions in Great Britain and the Empire, with the exception of Egypt and India; a proportion of the profits was to go to charities nominated by the War Office, with the remainder distributed among the members. After the deal was concluded a number of other film companies wanted to come on board but were firmly squashed by Brooke Wilkinson. The only exception was Charles Urban, whose experience was useful to the Committee as he had sent cameramen to film both the Boer War and the Russo-Japanese War. Urban tried to get the War Office to use his Kinemacolor system but they would not agree; it is tantalising to think that *The Battle of the Somme* could have been shot in colour.[2]

   The two cameramen were Geoffrey Malins and Edward 'Teddy' Tong. Geoffrey Malins was born Arthur Herbert Malins in Hastings in 1886 and had started his career as a portrait photographer before becoming a feature film cameraman with the Clarendon Film Company. In 1914 he moved to Gaumont and worked on 'topicals'. By October 1915 he had filmed successfully on both the Belgian and French sectors of the Western Front and thus was an obvious choice for the post.

*Ernest 'Baby' Brooks (left) and Geoffrey Malins at a coffee stall on the Western Front.*
(IWM Q1456)

*Geoffrey Malins (far right) wearing the War Office kinematographer's brassard. The occasion is the visit of the Prime Minister of New Zealand to 8 Squadron RNAS at Vert Galland in October 1916.* (IWM Q11846)

The other 'operator' was Edward 'Teddy' Tong, the factory manager for Jury's Imperial Pictures. They departed for the front on 2 November 1915 but Tong had to be evacuated back to England at Christmas and Malins continued working on his own. The footage was edited into six sets of short newsreels which were shown from January to July 1916 without a great amount of success. The quality of these films was variable but some, such as *Destruction of a German blockhouse*, were spectacular and involved immense risk to the cameraman. Others like *Letter from home: the work of the Postal Department at the front* failed to capture the popular imagination. Control over the footage was exercised by Captain John Faunthorpe as Military Director of Kinematography at GHQ I(d). Faunthorpe had previously been in the Indian Civil Service and was described by his successor Neville Lytton as 'a famous sportsman and a most charming man'.[3] He also had responsibility for the war correspondents, with whom he was very popular. Arrangements at the London end of the operation were overseen by Dr Edmund Distin Maddick, who began his career as a surgeon in the Royal Navy. By 1914 he owned the Scala Theatre, which was a fashionable venue for film premières. Charles Urban, who was originally from Illinois, was an early pioneer of colour film and a naturalised Briton. He was responsible for the acquisition of cameras and equipment but had fallen out with Distin Maddick over business and their relationship was 'none too friendly'.[4]

By the spring of 1916 the Committee was unhappy with the quality of the films which were not the commercial success they had hoped for. Some members, believing that restrictions on the movements of the cameramen made it impossible for them to do their job, wanted to withdraw from the agreement. Additionally there was tension within the Committee, many of whose members were commercial rivals. The War Office was eventually able to use this as an excuse to put an end to the arrangement and bring filming under much closer control in 1917. In June 1916 'Teddy' Tong was invalided home again and at a Committee meeting on 23 June 1916 one of the directors of British and Colonial, John Benjamin McDowell, volunteered to replace him on the Western Front.

McDowell was born in Plumstead in south London in 1878. He was christened Benjamin John McDowell but called himself John Benjamin throughout his life, although he was often known as 'Mac'. His father worked at Woolwich Arsenal and he started out as an apprentice there but later obtained a job as a cameraman for the British Mutoscope and Biograph Syndicate. He went into partnership with Albert Bloomfield, who had set up the British and Colonial Kinematograph Company. 'B&C', as it was usually known, initially made newsreels and McDowell filmed events such as the funeral of Edward VII, the Cup Final and the Derby. He also produced a feature epic entitled *The Battle of Waterloo*, probably the most ambitious and expensive British film up to that time. It stretched the company financially but turned out

*'Mac' McDowell (second left) with Ernest Brooks (third left). The other two men cannot be identified with any certainty.* (Kevin Brownlow)

to be a major success. As one interview stated, 'when the B and C Company were busily engaged on their great spectacular production of *The Battle of Waterloo* down in Northamptonshire three years ago, I don't suppose that the idea ever entered Mr J.B. McDowell's head that one day in the near future he would find himself taking part in "the real thing" in an official capacity'.[5] He was a member of the Topical Committee, an experienced cameraman, producer and film company executive and, while he had not filmed in combat before, he was in no sense subordinate to Malins.

Ernest Brooks accompanied Geoffrey Malins during the filming on the Somme. Known as 'Baby' because of his youthful appearance, he was an experienced press photographer. He had covered the royal tour of India in 1911 and knew the royal family, having spent his childhood on the Windsor estate. He had worked as a photographer at Gallipoli and had helped Ashmead Bartlett take some ciné film of that campaign.

CHAPTER THREE

# CINÉ FILM AND CAMERAS: THE TECHNICAL BACKGROUND

Any analysis of the work of McDowell and Malins involves an understanding of the technical capabilities and limitations of the equipment that they were using.[1] The capture and projection of moving images became a practical technology from the 1890s onwards. Cinematography grew from advances in still photography. Both work by allowing light to fall on to a flat surface treated with a light-sensitive substance. The resultant chemical reaction becomes visible by immersion in a bath of chemicals (developing) and is then made permanent (fixing). Because of the limitations of the early light-sensitive chemicals, called emulsions, exposure times were measured in minutes. By the late 1880s gelatine bromide emulsions reduced this to a fraction of a second. Film manufacturers were also able to produce a transparent, flexible and robust base made of celluloid which could be coated with the new emulsions and would stand the stresses of the exposure process. When perforated with sprocket holes strips of celluloid film could be drawn swiftly past a lens, each opening of the shutter recording a slightly different image as the film stopped briefly in front of it. After processing, the picture on the exposed film was visible in negative. Any unwanted footage was cut out and the film spliced into the required order before being printed on to another reel of film resulting in a set of positive images. Projection has to replicate the same intermittent motion and the same running speed as was used during exposure. The positive film, when passed frame by frame in front of a strong light source and projected on to a surface, created the illusion of movement.

The film in use in 1916 was made from cellulose nitrate, a derivative of wood pulp. Nitrate film is strong and relatively cheap to produce but has two major faults; being chemically similar to gun cotton, it is highly inflammable and cannot be extinguished even by immersion in water. The other characteristic is that it decomposes and eventually becomes unusable. The fumes released during this process can cause spontaneous combustion, making the storage of early film difficult. This only became clear in the 1940s when some stock was already half a century old. The phenomenon was of little interest to the cinema industry in 1916, which was generally intent only on maximising the profit from its productions. Heavily used prints often became badly damaged only months after issue and many were scrapped to recover the silver content in the emulsion. By the latter half of the twentieth century much surviving early film had decayed or was too volatile to keep. Despite the success of *The Battle of the Somme*, there is only one group of copies in existence that can confidently be linked directly back to the original. These all derive from a negative, believed to have been the original, reassembled in 1917 after some of it had been used in other films and transferred to the Imperial War Museum. The Museum possessed two other copies, including one on 1916 dated stock that may have been the original release, but these were destroyed when they became unstable during the 1950s or 1960s.[2]

The cameramen used 35mm orthochromatic film which is sensitive to the blue and green areas of the spectrum. While it was an improvement on earlier emulsions which only registered blue light, it was not as effective as panchromatic film which also recorded the red areas. Panchromatic film was produced before the Great War but required total darkness in the handling and developing processes, unlike 'ortho' film which could be worked on in red light as it was not sensitive to that wavelength. However, some elements of a picture, especially those in the red area of the spectrum, did not register very effectively on orthochromatic film. Particularly noticeable is the lack of detail in the sky: clouds did not photograph well. The contrast between light and dark areas of the image tends to be stark and there is little graduation of tone in shadows. Events were often fast moving and difficult to follow, the angle of the lens was fairly small, cameras were bulky, light could change or fade, and mechanical failures could occur. Focusing was normally set up before shooting and exposure was regulated by altering the shutter blade so that more or less light was admitted when the shutter opened. Most cameras had no view finder and keeping the subject in shot was a matter of experience and skill. The filming of combat included all these problems, with the addition of mortal danger. Comparison of the efforts of Ashmead Bartlett and Brooks in the Dardanelles as seen in their film *Heroes of Gallipoli* with those of Malins and McDowell on the Somme gives a clear impression of the difference a skilled cameraman could make. Ashmead Bartlett could not even do a pan without making the camera shake in some cases! Assuming a safe camera position with a good field of vision, there was often not a lot to see. Smoke and shell bursts were commonplace but difficult to film. Ironically the development of moving pictures coincided with the arrival of the 'empty battlefield'. Thus when filmed from any distance, attacking troops were no more than dots and defending troops were almost always invisible. Telephoto lenses were used in the Boer War but there is no evidence that Malins or McDowell had them.

Film was supplied in circular tin cans and was transferred to the film magazine using a changing bag. The film and the magazine were put into the lightproof, fabric bag and the operator removed the film from its tin and wound it on to the spool in the magazine entirely by feel. Exposed film was removed from the magazine and replaced in the tin by the same method; nicks or holes were often made in the film with scissors

*Malins using a Debrie camera with the characteristic rear-mounted film counter. This photograph is the frontispiece to his book and is captioned as having been taken on the Somme.* (Malins)

or a film punch to indicate the end of shots. The logistics of McDowell and Malins' operation are unclear. The normal procedure during newsreel filming was for exposed film to be sent back shortly after it had been taken so that the cameramen would get feedback on whether it had come out and what shots still needed to be filmed. Such evidence as there is seems to indicate that the film was sent back in one consignment on or about 10 July. In an interview given on that date McDowell certainly did not know if his 1 July footage had come out, something he would surely have been aware of if the film had been returned to London in batches.[3]

Malins began his film career in the Great War using an Aeroscope camera. This was a relatively light and portable design powered by compressed air but there were doubts about its reliability, although Bertram Brooks Carrington believed that it was fine if looked after carefully. Malins may have used a Debrie camera, a French design, for some of his filming on the Somme, while McDowell used the larger British Moy and Bastie, described below. Photographs taken by Ernest Brooks at White City and La Boisselle show Malins also using what looks like a Moy and Bastie rather than the smaller Debric. Both types were hand cranked and, unlike the Aeroscope, needed a tripod which hindered mobility. It seems that when Malins went to Advanced GHQ on 2 July he picked up his Aeroscope with the intention of using both cameras but near La Boisselle he lost the assistant who was carrying the Aeroscope and he probably continued using the Moy and Bastie.

The Moy and Bastie was a standard 'upright' camera consisting of a rectangular mahogany box subdivided along its long axis into two light-proof compartments, accessible by doors on each side. The door on the left side gave access to the film magazines and the lens mechanism. The right-hand compartment contained the drives for the film, the shutter and the intermittent mechanism. The cameraman carried several pre-loaded magazines of up to 400 feet which provided over six minutes of film; a magazine change could be carried out in a minute or so by an experienced cameraman

*A Moy and Bastie camera at the National Media Museum.*

*'Mac' McDowell with a Moy and Bastie ciné camera. This photograph appeared in* Kinematograph and Lantern Weekly *on 13 July 1916 and therefore represents his appearance on the Somme. He is dressed as an officer without rank or regimental badges. The 'head' mechanism which traversed and elevated the camera can be seen on the tripod. Using the left hand for the movement while maintaining a steady two revolutions per second with the right hand was not as difficult as it seemed and came with practice.* (Kevin Brownlow)

and film consumption was monitored by a counter. Power to operate the camera mechanism was supplied by the hand crank which drove a chain and a series of cogs. Standard 35mm film was designed to be exposed at 16 frames per second. As one revolution of the crank moved eight frames the cameraman had to complete two revolutions per second, although slightly faster or slower speeds were sometimes used depending on the light. Brooks Carrington said 'hand cranking came naturally. Purely automatic even under shellfire.'[4]

Photographs exist from earlier in 1916 showing Malins using a Parvo camera which was first manufactured in 1908 by Joseph Jules Debrie. This was a rectangular wooden box built round a metal frame which ran from front to rear, on which were mounted the mechanisms and film magazines. The sides had rearward opening doors and the front panel hinged upwards for access, and although the basic principle was similar to the Moy and Bastie it had some extras, including a film counter on the back rather than the side, a spirit level for accurate placement of the tripod and a revolution counter which could be set to either 16 or 24 revolutions per second to assist with exposing the film at a constant speed.

CHAPTER FOUR

# MALINS BETWEEN
# 25 AND 29 JUNE 1916

The principal source for the movements of Geoffrey Malins (and by inference Ernest Brooks) is Malins' *How I filmed the war*. The pass reproduced in the book was issued at 86 Brigade Headquarters on 27 June 1916 in Mailly-Maillet. Using this to assign dates to his activities and matching his descriptions to known events at the end of June, it emerges that Malins managed to miss an entire day, probably 30 June, out of his account. As he was operating under conditions of extreme stress and danger this is understandable. Malins appears to have been based at Montreuil in late June and knew from the atmosphere that something big was about to happen.

He recalled how he had a conversation with a colonel who announced that his 'chance to make history was coming'. Later the same day, probably 25 or 26 June, he was given instructions by a captain to move to the front line. More than likely the captain was Faunthorpe, who was his immediate boss. Malins seems to suggest that he set off on his own but the party was larger and included the photographer Ernest Brooks, their Army Service Corps driver David Laing and possibly Faunthorpe himself. Cameramen were normally accompanied by a conducting officer who was supposed to advise on what might be filmed. Some shots, all taken by Malins after 2 July, show a tall officer in a trench coat who may be the conducting officer. The party had at least one and possibly two cars which appear in various scenes.

David Laing was an Army Service Corps driver who normally drove ambulances but in 1916 he was seconded to act as driver to Malins and Brooks. He was 20 years old and had joined the army in May 1915. Laing, writing in 1964, remarked of Malins: 'Although I was his driver, I had to take him out as far as we were allowed in daylight, and then take to the communications lines up to the front, as he carried the tripod and I the camera and changed over occasionally as they were both quite heavy compared to the present day ones.'[1]

The party set off for what Malins calls 'the section facing Gouerment', a garbled rendering of Gommecourt. En route, they came across a battalion of the London Scottish. The battalion had been relieved in the front line on 21 June and was in a hutted camp at Pas-en-Artois. Malins describes seeing them being addressed by a general. The battalion took part in a large exercise on 26 June around Hurtebise

*In a letter to Tony Essex, the editor of the television series* The Great War, *Laing described this photograph which was taken 'about November 1916 when Jerry evacuated the line on a [length] of about thirty miles, and a likewise depth going back to the Hindenburg Line*

*. . . We called in at a house where an old couple lived and had been under German rule for two years. They had no fuel for the stove except what they could gather from the woods, they were very scant of food, with black-looking bread and very little meat. We returned the next day. My two bosses took up some French loaves and sausages etc. also a copy of* Le Petit Journal *to give the old couple the latest news. Mr Brooks took a flash-light photograph inside the house.' Laing is on the left wearing a driver's leather coat. The two other men, according to Laing, are from the Royal Engineers Special Brigade.*
(IWM 1900)

Farm, near the village of Halloy, in the presence of the Third Army and VII Corps commanders, Sir Edmund Allenby and Sir Thomas D'Oyly Snow, and it is very likely that the existing footage and related stills were taken on that day.[2]

**Date: 26 June 1916? Place: north-west outskirts of Pas-en-Artois. Description: pipe band and A Company 1 London Scottish, 168 Brigade, 56 Division. Shots: 14.1 and 14.2. Stills: DH40. Q790–793. Cameraman: Malins.**

Four stills of the London Scottish exist in the IWM collections, all dated July 1916. The date on each has been altered in manuscript, presumably on the advice of a veteran, to 'June 27, near Pas-en-Artois', but it is more likely that they were taken on 26 June. The ciné footage can be precisely located and shows the pipe band and what is probably A Company. The derelict gatepost on the left in shots 14.1–2 is still in the hedgerow and pinpoints Malins' camera position precisely.

The manuscript annotations on Q790 identify members of the pipe band and the company that appears in shot 14.1. The officer leading A Company is Captain H.C. Sparks. The other men are Pipe Major W.P. Keith, Pipers A. Foulis, W.W. Zambra,

R.D. Marshall, A.A. Connell and R. Gordon, Drummers J.A. Hall, J.H. Ridsdale, D.S. Middleton and R.W. Somerville. All these men survived the war with the exception of Piper Alan Connell, the middle man in the second rank. Connell was from Oban and died on 29 September 1916. He is buried in Neuville Cemetery at Corbie. Trained pipers were hard to come by and were generally kept out of battle by this stage of the war. Piper Warren Zambra, who is the right-hand man in the front rank, was born in 1898 and educated at Chatham House School and Christ's College, Cambridge. Commissioned later in the war, he ended his military career as a colonel and was awarded the CVO and CBE. He changed his name to Shaw-Zambra in 1925. After the war he went into telecommunications and was involved in the founding of the Royal Ballet School. Also a governor of the Royal Ballet until 1968, he died on 25 March 1971 at the age of 73.[3]

The two officers marching immediately behind the pipes and drums are believed to be Lieutenant Allan Grant Douglas and Captain Frederick George Worlock. The annotations are somewhat ambiguous and Alan MacDonald in his *Pro patria mori* suggests that the right-hand man may be Lieutenant H.C. Lamb. Allan Douglas from Farley House, Westerham, Kent, appears to be the officer on the left. He enlisted in the London Scottish as a private in September 1914, served at Messines and was commissioned in early 1915. In September 1916 he was appointed adjutant, a rank he held until his death in action during the Battle of Cambrai on 30 November 1917. He is buried in Mouevres Communal Cemetery.[4]

Frederick Worlock was born in London in 1886 and was an actor with F.R. Benson's theatre company from 1908. He left the stage at the outbreak of war and was commissioned in the London Scottish in May 1915. He spent 1 July in the front line and survived unscathed but while commanding A Company was seriously wounded by a shell on 28 May 1917. This caused him to be invalided out of the army and he resumed his acting career, appearing in *Violette* at the Lyric Theatre in May 1918. His wife divorced him in 1919 but he continued working in the West End until 1922, when he moved to the United States. On Broadway in 1923 he met the silent film star Elsie Ferguson, whom he married the following year. Sadly this marriage only survived until 1930. He reappeared briefly on the stage in London in 1936 but is perhaps better known as a regular performer in the series of films produced by Universal which starred Basil Rathbone and Nigel Bruce as Sherlock Holmes and Dr Watson respectively. His last film role was as the voice of Cruella De Vil's incompetent henchman Horace Badun in Walt Disney's *One hundred and one Dalmatians*. He continued to work in television until 1968 and died in Hollywood in 1973.[5]

Hubert Conrad Sparks was born on 14 February 1874. His family lived at Putney Hill in London and Hubert went to Repton School before becoming an electrical engineer. He joined the London Scottish as a private in February 1900 and by 1914 was a sergeant. Surviving Messines, he was commissioned as a second lieutenant on 19 December 1914 but was shot in the right thigh two days later. He returned to the battalion in March 1915 and by June 1916 had been awarded the MC. He was

*Q790 and Q791 were taken by Brooks from the balcony of a house slightly further along the village. Malins is probably obscured by the nearer of two cars parked on the right side of the road.* (IWM Q790–791)

*The same view in 2007.*

*The old gatepost on the left fixes shots 14.1–2.*

described in a confidential report in May 1916 as an 'exceptionally capable and careful officer'.

On 1 July Captain Sparks and his company were on the extreme right of the diversionary assault by 56 Division on the village of Gommecourt. By about 4pm Sparks was in command of all the men remaining in the German lines and managed to get a message back which read:

> I am faced with this position. I have collected all SAA and bombs from casualties. Every one has been used. Owing to the enemy's continued barrage fire no more can be brought to me. I am faced with three alternatives – A) to stay here with such of my men as are alive, and be killed. B) to surrender to the enemy. C) to withdraw such of my men as I can. Either of the first two alternatives is distasteful to me. I propose to adopt the latter.

The wounded were got away first and then the remaining fit men. As they escaped across no-man's-land Captain Sparks and some NCOs remained on the German parapet with a Lewis gun to cover the withdrawal. Trapped in a shell hole 50 yards from the German lines Sparks only got back four hours later. He was awarded the DSO and became successively Assistant Director of Labour and Labour Commandant for Third Army, although he suffered from neurasthenia, probably resulting from his ordeal at Gommecourt. He was demobilised in January 1919 with a CMG. He remained in the Territorial Force Reserve after the war and returned to his engineering practice, also being an enthusiastic supporter of the British Legion. He retired from the Army in 1929 and died after an operation on 15 October 1933. His obituary in *The Times* summed him up as 'a very gallant Christian gentleman'.[6]

The London Scottish Regimental Museum has identified the officer behind the stretcher-bearers in Q791 as Second Lieutenant Herbert Archibald Coxon. He was born in Gravesend in Kent in 1884 and worked as a financial agent. He had been in Victoria, British Columbia, but returned to enlist at the beginning of the war. He was an acting sergeant with 3 London Scottish by November 1914 and was commissioned in November of the following year. He had only been in France since 3 April 1916 and was killed by shellfire on 1 July. Like those of so many of his comrades, his name is on the Thiepval memorial.[7]

The men of the London Scottish wear a mixture of 1908 and 1914 pattern equipment. The owners of the 1908 pattern sets could be 'originals' and those wearing 1914 pattern may be reinforcements. Most men have helmet covers and some also have a tuft of material on the left side of the helmet. The ciné sequence was shot in two sections. Malins stopped filming after the first rank of A Company approached the camera and began again as the last company and the battalion transport appeared. Marching at the rear of the column are the battalion stretcher-bearers, with their SB armbands, first aid bags and stretchers. Among them, identifiable by the Red Cross roundel on his upper sleeve, is one of the attached RAMC orderlies. Note also the Scottish lion rampant flag that appears very briefly at the beginning of 14.2. Whether this was an officially sanctioned identification or a privately owned flag is unknown. One of the stretcher-bearers in the file furthest away from the camera can be tentatively identified as Private John Christopher Lander. It is unclear when Lander went to France but he served as a stretcher-bearer and his regimental number 6074 is close to those of a number of fatal casualties on 1 July. He was killed in action at Cambrai on 24 November 1917. Another member of the battalion, Thomas Holmes, later wrote in a letter home of Lander's death:

> Our dresser, Lander, went out to dress the wounds of a man in the open, and whilst administering to him was shot in the lower part of the body and legs. He administered morphia to himself to deaden the pain and stretcher-bearers went out to fetch him in. 'Let me finish with this man and then take him, he is worse than I am.' They brought in the other man and then returned for Lander, but he was dead. Lander was a fine man and went through the previous Balkan wars in the Red Cross Ambulance.

This very brave man has no known grave and is commemorated on the Cambrai memorial.[8]

Two men in Q793 can be identified. The first appears in the file nearest the camera and has a wristwatch visible. This is 6248 Private Douglas Shuker, aged 20, who was from Audlem in Cheshire. He was killed on 1 July and is buried in Gommecourt

*Private John Christopher Lander of Betsom's Farm, Westerham, Kent.* (London Scottish Regimental Gazette)

*Q792 and Q793 may have been taken as the battalion returned from its final exercise in the Hurtebise Farm area. They may be marching down the D5 which joins the D26 on the north-west edge of Pas-en-Artois. The original caption reads: 'London Scottish marching to the trenches; near Doullens–Amiens road, July 1916.'* (IWM Q792–793)

*Private John Henry Dunbar with members of his family prior to embarking for France.* (London Scottish Regimental Museum)

British Cemetery no. 2. In the same rank to Shuker's right is a taller soldier known to be 5638 Private John Henry Dunbar. He was born in 1883, lived in Bow and worked as a highways inspector in the East End of London. He enlisted on 22 November 1915 and joined 1 London Scottish on 24 May 1916. He was more fortunate than Shuker; although he was shot in the thigh on 1 July he survived to be evacuated back to England. The wound was serious enough to ensure that he was discharged as medically unfit on 24 April 1917.[9]

**Date: 26 June 1916? Place: near Vauchelles? Description: 10 East Yorks on the march. Shot: 14.3. Stills: DH44–45, Q724, Q743, IWM FLM 1657. Cameraman: Malins?**

The dope sheet dates this shot to 26 June but the history of 10 East Yorks claims that it was in fact filmed on 3 July when the commanding officer, Lieutenant Colonel W.B. Pearson, took the battalion out on a route march and encountered the cameraman near Vauchelles. Despite this seemingly convincing evidence, we found the story slightly unlikely. His predecessor, Lieutenant Colonel Daniel Burges, was replaced on 30 June for unknown reasons. Comparison of the admittedly poor image of the mounted officer in the film with photographs of Burges and Pearson suggest that it is probably Burges and that the footage was shot before 1 July as the dope sheet says. Burges went on to win the VC in 1918.[10]

*10 East Yorks in a screen grab and still captioned 'near Doullens: 28 June 1916'.*
(IWM FLM 1657 and Q724)

*Q743 is said by the battalion history to have been taken at the same time as the ciné footage. It shows 15 Platoon of D Company and is dated '3 July 1916'.*
(IWM Q743)

*12-inch howitzer from shots 19.1–5, possibly at Humbercamps.*
(DH53)

**Date: 26–27 June 1916? Place: Humbercamps? Description: 12-inch railway gun being fired. Shots: 19.1–5. Stills: DH53–54, Q40, Q43, Q876. Cameraman: Malins.**

These shots show a 12-inch railway gun being loaded and fired with a fine disregard for the hearing of the crew. The piece may be the 12-inch howitzer of 103 Siege Battery which was positioned on a railway spur on the outskirts of Humbercamps. Stills of this piece are dated 1 July, which is probably too late, and the dope sheet gives 25 June, which is too early. It is possible that the footage was taken on 26 or 27 June. However, there is nothing conclusive to link the ciné footage with the howitzer in the stills and it may be significant that the chalk-board that one of the crew writes on bears the legend 'Fricourt napoo' on the reverse, which might place it much further south.

## 27 June 1916

If Malins is correct about his movements on the evening of 26 June, they returned to 'GHQ', which may be Chateau Val Vion in Beauquesne, occupied as Haig's Advanced GHQ on 25 June. They received orders to report to 'a certain division', which was 29 Division. On 27 June they presumably started from Beauquesne, filmed the 88 Brigade exercise near Louvencourt, went up to Souastre to film the 9.2-inch howitzer and probably then travelled back south to Acheux. Malins describes a meeting there with a general, almost certainly General Beauvoir de Lisle of 29 Division. It is possible that he also filmed the ammunition dump north of the town at this time. After reporting to 86 Brigade headquarters in the Café Jourdan in Mailly-Maillet they went to the front-line trenches at White City between Beaumont Hamel and Auchonvillers. Between 4 and 6pm Malins filmed the bombardment of Beaumont Hamel, which appears in the missing footage of caption 20.

**Date: 27 June 1916. Place: about 750m north-east of Louvencourt. Description: 2 Hants and 4 Worcesters of 88 Brigade, 29 Division on the Louvencourt training area. Shots: 10.5, 10.6, 22.1, 22.2, 61.1. Stills: DH31, DH58, DH162, Q716–719, Q740, Q1459, Q79482, IWM FLM 1649. Cameraman: Malins.**

Malins and Brooks filmed troops of 88 Brigade on the Louvencourt training area. Malins makes no reference to this in his book and some footage is wrongly described in the film and on the dope sheet. Sources for the date are contradictory but the battalions shown are 2 Hampshire Regiment and 4 Worcestershire Regiment. The training area consisted of a reproduction of the German trench system which was laid out using a plough by Lieutenant Hall of 2 Hants.[11] On Tuesday 27 June there was a brigade exercise, described as being a rehearsal of 'the final stage of the advance and assault from the Station Road to the third German line'.[12] This suggests that 27 June is almost certainly the correct date, despite Q718 and Q719 being dated 28 June 1916.

*This grab shows shot 10.6 with 2 Hants marching off the training area in the direction of Louvencourt. The two identifiers are the windmill on the skyline at left and the tin triangles with a vertical strip which denoted 88 Brigade, 29 Division. These are described as being 'a tin triangular disc with a red line on obverse and reverse sides from apex to centre of base of the triangle'.[13]* (IWM Q79482)

*The same view in 2007 with the windmill in the trees on the horizon. Now without sails, it stands to the north of the village on the right side of the road to Authie.*

*The original caption reads: 'The 4 Battalion of the Worcestershire Regiment (29
Division) resting, on their way to the trenches. Note wire cutters attached to rifles;
Acheux, 29 June, 1916.' The white armbands worn by the corporal on the left and the
sergeant in the centre identify them as carrying conventional wire cutters, a pair of which
can be seen between the sergeant's legs. The men have their regimental badge stencilled or
painted on the front of their helmets, a common practice on the Somme in 1916. They
wear the famous half-diamond or 'bottle of Bass' patch of 29 Division. (IWM Q718)*

*This photo is taken from further back with the Bois de Warnimont in the background.*
(IWM Q719)

*The position from which shot 10.5 was filmed, with the Bois de Warnimont on the skyline and the shallow Vallée des Trieze on the left. It shows 2 Hants marching past the camera, but no still or screen grab exists.*

*4 Worcesters as recorded by Ernest Brooks.* (IWM Q716–717)

*Captioned as the Wiltshire Regiment on 28 June near Acheux, this photograph was probably taken at the same time and may be 4 Worcesters. (IWM Q740)*

*Men of 4 Worcestershire Regiment (88 Brigade, 29 Division) resting near Aveluy, September 1916. There is some doubt about the date as 29 Division was in the Ypres Salient in September. Whatever the location, these men look very far from the confident and cheerful figures seen in Q716 and 717. (IWM Q1459)*

Shot 61.1 is captioned 'SEEKING FURTHER LAURELS. A "SAMPLE" OF THE BRITISH ARMY (THE WORCESTERS) OFF TO CONTINUE THE ADVANCE', which is incorrect. The background indicates that it was taken on the training area and is contemporary with the earlier sequences. Brooks took Q716 and Q717 slightly to the right of Malins showing the same column of troops. The men have just been issued with sandbags which most have pushed through their belts. Contrast their appearance Q1459 which shows the battalion in September 1916.

**Date: 27 June 1916? Place: on the slope of a valley to the west of Bayencourt. Description: 9.2-inch howitzer in action. Shots: 17.1–2. Still: DH49. Cameraman: Malins.**

Shots 17.3–6 are discussed in Chapter 10. The first two shots show a 9.2-inch breech-loading Mark I siege howitzer on the slope of a valley. There is a telescope on the skyline with which it would be possible to see the fall of shot in the German lines around Gommecourt. The dope sheet allocates this footage to Malins 'near Albert' on 27 June 1916. The howitzer is emplaced on the steep western slope of the valley known as Les Cailloux west of Bayencourt. The valley lies within the VII Corps area and the three 9.2-inch howitzer batteries of 47 Heavy Artillery Group were around Bayencourt, about 1,500 yards to the east. Their target was mainly the German lines

*The 9.2-inch howitzer being loaded. Notice the counterweight box in front of the piece to prevent it rearing up as it fired.* (DH49)

*A still taken from almost the same position as shot 9.2 and probably at about the same time, with a comparison photograph taken in 2007. Note the boxes and empty shell cases lining the left side of the road. Shot 9.3 shows a larger pile of empties which would eventually be refilled in England. (IWM Q735)*

around Gommecourt, with an additional allocation of ammunition for counter-battery work. The most probable candidate is 95 Siege Battery but that unit's war diary has not survived so the identity remains unconfirmed.

**Date: 27 June 1916? Place: 29 Division ammunition dump north of Acheux. Description: gun and mortar ammunition being unloaded and distributed. Shots: 8.1–3, 9.2–3, 9.4–5, 15.1–3. Stills: DH22, DH24, DH26, DH32, DH46, DH48, Q727, Q735, Q747, Q749. Cameraman: Malins.**

The emphasis of this footage is to demonstrate how vital munitions were to the war effort. Shot 8.1, which we cannot trace, shows a large dump, probably of artillery ammunition. Shots 8.2–3, 9.2–3 and 15.1–3 were all filmed at the 29 Division ammunition dump which was in an orchard just north of Acheux.[14] The dope sheet merely gives a date between 25 and 30 June although Q727 is captioned '4 July', which seems unlikely. The footage in the three captions is clearly linked, and as Malins had lunch with De Lisle in Acheux on 27 June it is likely that it was filmed that day. The motorcycle combination and the four lorries, possibly Albions, have come from the centre of Acheux and turned left into the dump. As the following shot shows a lorry being unloaded they have probably come from the ammunition railhead at Puchevillers, which supplied 29 Division. Divisional dumps stored ammunition for 18-pounders and 4.5-inch howitzers as well as trench mortars. Ammunition for heavier guns was

*These bombs have no sandbag walls or protection. The accidental detonation of a single round would be catastrophic.* (IWM Q749)

*Men carrying 2-inch mortar bombs to transport on the road. A short and very portly officer and an equally well fed but taller staff sergeant can be seen in the background. They appear prominently in shot 15.3. The 29 Divisional Ammunition Column was formed from 53 (Welsh) Divisional Ammunition Column in April 1916 and it is probable that both men were from this unit.*
(IWM Q747)

*Ammunition being loaded into a GS wagon at the dump.* (IWM Q727)

*The site of the dump in 2007.*

supplied by corps dumps. The crated ammunition seen here is stored in tarpaulin shelters before the boxes are opened and the shells distributed to the limbers and wagons of the batteries. Shot 9.2 and Q735 show empty cases being dumped and fresh ammunition, apparently shrapnel shells, lying on the ground ready to be loaded. Batteries of both 29 and 48 Division drew from this dump.

Shots 9.4–5 show boxes being levered open and a chain of gunners loading shrapnel shells into limbers. The man opening the boxes is exclaiming 'Get them open' as he works. These shots were not taken at the dump near Acheux. The terrain does not match that area and despite the clues in the background the location has eluded us.

The dump also supplied bombs, referred to in the caption as 'plum puddings', for the divisional 2-inch mortars. Shots 15.1–3 show these being taken from a huge pile and carried away by Royal Artillery personnel.

## The Missing Caption 20

The footage for caption 20 is no longer in the existing print. Malins describes how he took it but it was later removed for some reason and the only evidence for it seems to be a screen grab in *Sir Douglas Haig's great push* and a mention in the dope sheet which gives it the caption 'CONTINUOUS SHELL FIRE FOR FIVE DAYS OVER BEAUMONT

*The original caption from* Sir Douglas Haig's great push *reads: 'a view taken from the British trenches showing a shell bursting over Beaumont Hamel. Here shells were fired continuously day and night for five days previous to the Great Push.' This sequence was taken from Lanwick Street trench near Jacob's Ladder to the north of the New Beaumont Road in the 1 Lancashire Fusiliers' front-line trenches and shows a heavy shell exploding at the north end of Beaumont Hamel. The line of trees on the horizon matches Malins' description of a 'few remaining stumps of trees, which used to be a beautiful wood, near which the village nestled'. The trees nearer the camera are those in the sunken lane in no-man's-land.* (DH57)

*The same view in 2007.*

HAMEL'. However, at least some of this footage still exists; comparison between the screen grab and two fragments from episode two of the Nugus/Martin Productions *World War One in colour* shows that all three are from the same sequence. The original black and white footage has been traced in a compilation of material entitled *Our*

*Empire's fight for freedom* (IWM Film and Video Archive 440/6). A number of other missing shots are discussed elsewhere.

The dope sheet dates it to 23 June 1916 but Malins was not in France then and the sequence fits exactly with his description of events on the afternoon of 27 June 1916. De Lisle informed him that there would be a bombardment of Beaumont Hamel at 4pm which he could film. He arrived at what he described as the 'brigade dugout' at White City, which is more likely to have been the 1 Lancashire Fusiliers HQ. In conversation with the occupants Malins told them how he had 'come this afternoon to look round, and to film the "strafe" at Beaumont Hamel'. Lanwick Street was recommended to him and on arriving there he 'looked out on the village, or rather the late site of it. It was absolutely flattened out.' An artillery observation officer sharing the trench warned him to be careful. Malins continued: 'I chose a spot for working and fixed up my tripod, and waited until 4.30pm', half an hour later than de Lisle had stated. He disguised his camera with a piece of sacking and wrapped a khaki handkerchief round his hand.

> The first of the 15-inch came over and exploded with a deafening roar. The sight was stupefying. I began to expose my film, swinging the camera first to one side then the other. Shell after shell came roaring over; one dropped on the remaining walls of a château, and when the smoke had cleared there was absolutely nothing left. . . . I continued to expose my film at intervals until about 6 o'clock and twice I had to snatch my camera down hastily and take shelter, for the 'whizz-bangs' came smashing too close for safety.

Documentary corroboration is found in the VIII Corps war diary which mentions a 'special bombardment task' which was carried out between 4.30 and 6.00pm on 27 June.[15]

**Date: 27–30 June. Place: not located. Description: four gun battery in covered positions. Shot: 9.1. Still: DH25. Cameraman: Malins.**
This is another shot with few clues and we have not traced it. War diaries emphasise the amount of labour involved in constructing gun positions, although this is not clear from the film, where many guns have little in the way of protection.

## 28 June 1916

At this point Malins' chronology becomes confused. We know that 28 June was a day of very heavy rain; some scenes were filmed in these conditions and can be dated to that day, which he seems to have spent around the Mailly-Maillet area. He implies that he filmed the scenes of General Beauvoir de Lisle addressing troops during the morning but de Lisle's speech to 2 Royal Fusiliers, as recorded by Malins, states that the event had been postponed from the anniversary of the attack on Gully Ravine on 28 June 1915 because of the rain. This set of shots is described under 29 June.

*The shots of horses being watered at troughs show at least two men with 29 Division badges, which supports our interpretation. Royal Artillery cap badges can be seen in all the shots. (DH23)*

**Date: 28 June 1916. Place: near Mailly-Maillet. Description: horse lines in the rain and horses being watered. Shots: 7.2–5. Still: DH23. Cameraman: Malins.**

The first and last scenes in caption 7 were shot by McDowell. The scenes of horses in the open can be credited to Malins and demonstrate why the attack was postponed late on the morning of 28 June. Despite the woods visible in shots 7.2 and 7.3 it is impossible to find the locations although it is reasonable to assume that they are in the 29 Division back areas.

**Date: 28 June 1916. Place: Bois Dauville and Mailly Wood. Description: loading and firing two 15-inch howitzers. Shots: 25.1–14, 26.1–2. Stills: DH65–68, Q31–33, Q35, Q37, Q876–879, Q79489. Cameraman: Malins.**

All the 15-inch howitzers on the Western Front were crewed by the Royal Marine Artillery as they had originally been ordered by the Admiralty. Malins almost certainly filmed most of this footage on 28 June. It shows two of the eight pieces operational in June 1916. No. 1 howitzer was mounted at Mailly-Maillet in the valley to the east side of the Hedauville to Mailly-Maillet road, now the D919. No. 2 was at Mailly-Maillet but had a premature burst on 27 June which put it and no. 8 out of action. No. 5 is described as being at Engelbelmer but the war diary of the Commander Royal Artillery of X Corps puts it at the south edge of Bois Dauville on the west of the Hedauville to Mailly-Maillet road. It was only a few hundred yards from no. 1. and the dope sheet suggests a connection with X Corps as well. Although there were also two others at Souastre and one at Sailly au Bois and Albert, the fact that Malins describes the howitzers as being 'in the vicinity' strongly suggests that he filmed nos 1 and 5. He tells how: 'I filmed the firing several times, from various points of view, and when

*These are companion stills to shots 25.1–2. They were filmed in sunshine so cannot have been taken at the same time as the rest of this caption. There is no indication of the location.* (IWM Q876, Q879)

*A 15-inch howitzer in fine weather.* (IWM Q33)

*No. 1 howitzer firing.* (IWM Q79489)

*The position of no. 1 howitzer in 2007.*

standing only about fifteen yards away the concussion shook the ground like a miniature earthquake. On one occasion, indeed, it lifted my camera and tripod into the air, driving it crashing into my chest.' David Laing also remembered Malins being knocked over by the blast. The loading sequence appears to have been filmed at no. 1 howitzer as the terrain fits its stated position. The scenes in caption 26 were probably taken at no. 5 howitzer, although with only the wood in the background there are now no features for comparison.[16]

**Date: 30 June 1916? Place: Apple Trees, on the ridge south of the Sucrerie on the Mailly-Maillet to Serre Road. Description: Forward Observation Officer in trench; machine gunners mounting a gun and firing; two panoramas over the Ancre valley. Shots: FOO 30.1; machine gunners 30.2–3; panoramas 13.4, 30.4. Stills: FOO: DH77; machine gunners: DH74, Q79484; panoramas: DH80–81, Q79496–79497. Cameraman: Malins.**

Shot 30.1 shows a Royal Artillery officer observing through a loophole in an unstable-looking wall of sandbags with a Royal Garrison Artillery telephonist behind him. There are no clues as to location. Malins describes meeting an observation officer in Lanwick Street but there is nothing to show that this is him. There was an observation post near the Apple Trees from 1915 and it is possible that Malins filmed near there.[17]

The next four shots show men of the Machine Gun Corps getting a Vickers machine gun from a dugout and mounting the tripod on the parapet, and a further one shows

*A grab showing the trees at the north end of the sunken lane in front of Beaumont Hamel.* (IWM Q79484)

*The trees can be seen but an exact comparison was impossible in 2006.*

a Vickers in the sustained-fire role in a trench. Additionally the footage contains two panoramas over no-man's-land and shows British artillery shelling the German lines. Some doubt has been cast on the genuineness of these scenes but as the viewing notes point out, the guns had a range of nearly two miles and there was little danger.

The panoramas in shots 13.4 and 30.4 are of the same place and were filmed from the top of the ridge rising up from Auchonvillers to the Sucrerie, just north of the Mailly-Maillet to Serre road. The distinctive tree trunks in both shots indicate that they linked. The panorama in its two segments moves from Redan Ridge to Hawthorn Ridge and shows both British and German shellfire. The area of the present-day

Newfoundland Park is shown at the end of the second panorama, the only known film of this area. The ridge on the far side of the Ancre valley can just be made out. Much discussion has focused on how heavy the British bombardment actually was in the VIII Corps area and now we can see it happening. Shot 13.4 shows shrapnel detonating very high in the air; this was presumably intended to cut the wire, and demonstrates the difficulty of fuse setting and ranging. There are also several rounds of high explosive and a feature on fire within the German lines near the north end of the sunken lane. Shot 30.4 is a longer pan also showing the British trenches on Hawthorn Ridge as well as shellfire on the crest of the ridge.

The dope sheet states that the scenes in caption 13 were shot by Malins and dates them as 27 June. It gives the location as 'Albert Road' but this may refer to the footage of 60-pounders that precedes the panorama. We know from Malins that he was in the area on the afternoon of 27 June and used the Fifth Avenue communication trench to get to White City. Fifth Avenue is generally shown on trench maps as beginning on the sunken road from Auchonvillers to the Sucrerie in which both Malins and Brooks are known to have worked. Several British and German maps from after July 1916 show it extending up the hill towards the machine-gun positions. The location of these

*A screen grab from shot 30.3. The lance corporal firing the gun appears at the end of the previous shot walking from right to left across the camera. He has only just started firing the belt that is in place and may have a stoppage.* (IWM Q79496)

shots is a short walk up the hill along a present-day farm track. The date – 27 June – may be correct but the footage does not tally with Malins' description of the weather on that afternoon which he recalled as being 'like it is on a bad November day at home'. Artillery observation was seriously hampered by the conditions. In the photograph, however, terrain over 2,000 yards from the camera is identifiable and there is no evidence of rain. Although Malins used Fifth Avenue again on 28 June the weather had not improved and we can see what the conditions were like from his footage of the 15-inch howitzers. Tentatively we suggest that the panorama fits better with the conditions on 30 June.[18]

The two shots of the machine gunners were probably taken at the same time as the panoramas. The lance corporal seen in the photo on p.43 also appears in shots 30.2 and 30.3. He is identifiable by the hole in the left elbow of his tunic; the same man is also seen, this time wearing his steel helmet, at the end of shot 30.2, which would indicate that they were taken together. The terrain in 30.3 and 30.4 seems to be very similar.

Malins filmed machine gunners of 10 Brigade MGC cleaning their guns in shots 59.1 and 59.2 on 1 July but these are not the same men. In shot 30.2 the men are wearing service dress tunics and in some cases shorts. They have 1908 pattern equipment with ground sheets worn rolled in the small of their backs and have sacking helmet covers and MGC shoulder titles. The helmet covers would suggest that they are probably from one of the 4 Division brigade machine gun companies. The narrative

*A grab from the beginning of shot 30.4, the longer of the two panoramas.* (IWM Q79497)

in the 11 Brigade war diary notes that one section of 11 MGC was positioned on a line from Fifth Avenue to Elles Square on the morning of 30 June.[19] The guns that are filmed are at the bottom end of this line. We cannot say for certain that these are men of 11 Brigade MGC but the weather conditions certainly resemble those of 30 June rather better than either 27 or 28 June. Range tables give the maximum range of the Vickers machine gun as 2,800 yards and the tangent rear sight is graduated to 2,900 yards. The German front line is some 2,300 yards away and thus well within range.

*An unexploded 15-inch shell from one of the Royal Marine Artillery howitzers seen in captions 25 and 26. These were devastatingly effective when they were accurate and when they exploded. This example was intended to hit Grandcourt.*
(Von Holtz, 32)

The guns are probably laying down a barrage of harassing fire on the northern end of Beaumont Hamel or on Redan Ridge. The British front line was about 1,700 yards distant so within the safety margin for overhead fire which was set at 2,000 yards from the guns. These barrages were normally fired at night and were quite accurate. On the night of 28 June 119 Reserve Infanterie Regiment (RIR) recorded British machine guns firing on trench junctions.[20]

Although the bombardment looks impressive, how effective was it and what of the men enduring it? The sector was garrisoned by men of 121 RIR. The regimental boundary was just north of Beaumont Hamel, and the village itself and the trenches down to the banks of the River Ancre were occupied by their sister regiment, 119 RIR. Both regiments were part of 26 Reserve Division which was almost entirely recruited from Württemberg in southern Germany. The division had been in the area since September 1914 and was well trained and prepared. Modern research has emphasised the inadequacy of the artillery preparations for the battle but nevertheless being under British bombardment was an unpleasant experience. Heavy damage was done to the positions of 119 RIR on 30 June 1916; eight dugouts were destroyed, entrances blocked and communication trenches and barbed wire almost obliterated. Casualties were remarkably light and crucially the machine guns survived; from 24 June to the morning of 1 July the regiment lost twenty NCOs and men dead and sixty wounded, two of whom remained on duty. Five officers were wounded on 29 or 30 June but two stayed at their posts.[21]

The battle report of II/121 RIR remarked on the effects of the bombardment: 'Then the nerves consequently in those days were under great demands because it is not a pleasant situation when shot after shot follows, in the next instant the roof above you could engulf you.'[22] The positions of 121 RIR probably suffered more extensively from the bombardment than those of 119 RIR. The regimental battle headquarters in Soden Redoubt in the intermediate line suffered a direct hit and was heavily damaged. The commander of II/121 RIR, Captain Freiherr von Ziegesar, was seriously wounded by a British shell in Nagelgraben, just behind the front line, on 25 June and died in the early hours of the next morning, the only officer of the regiment killed during the bombardment. Total casualties for the period 24–30 June amounted to 24 dead, 122 wounded and one missing. This is comparable to the losses of 119 RIR, except for twice as many wounded. Both regiments were about 3,000 officers and men strong and after a week of the worst the British Army could throw at them they had lost only 227 from a total of nearly 6,000 men. They had sat in ill-ventilated dugouts, eating salty, tinned food and may have been tired, dirty, thirsty and running short of cigarettes, but most of them were still alive and keen to get their own back.[23]

## Filming in the Sunken Road

**Date: 30 June 1916? Place: the sunken road north-east of Auchonvillers. Description: dead soldier on stretcher being removed from trench and placed by the side of the road. Shots: 35.2–3. Stills: DH93–94, Q79502. Cameraman: Malins.**

The occupants of both stretchers appear to be dead. The shot was filmed in the sunken road to the north-east of Auchonvillers (not to be confused with the sunken lane in front of Beaumont Hamel), and the trench is Fifth Avenue. The trench name is visible on a signboard on the left of shot 35.2. Malins stated that he used Fifth Avenue to get to and from the front line. It may have been taken on the way to or from the machine-gun positions seen in caption 30, which was only some 300 yards to the west.

*Shots 35.2–3 show RAMC stretcher-bearers lifting a stretcher out of a trench, carrying it past the camera and putting it down next to another stretcher by the side of a road.*
(IWM Q79502)

*A screen grab showing the sunken road leading to the outskirts of Auchonvillers.* (DH94)

*The same stretch of road in 2007.*

*Several trench bridges can be seen in the background of 35.3 and identical bridges appear in Q60, which was taken early on 1 July over the rise in the background. The absence of troops in 35.3 suggests that the trenches had not yet been occupied. The survivors of 2 Seaforth Highlanders spent 2 July in these trenches so Malins did not film the scene on his way out of the line on that day.*
(IWM Q60)

## Trench Mortars

**Date: 29 June 1916. Place: Lanwick Street trench in the front line opposite Beaumont Hamel. Description: loading and firing a 2-inch trench mortar. Shots: 16.1–2. Stills: DH47, Q79486, IWM FLM 1653. Cameraman: Malins.**

Footage exists of both 2-inch and 9.45-inch trench mortars. Both of these types, together with the 3-inch Stokes mortar, formed an important part of the preparatory bombardment. The dope sheet gives a date of 29 June 1916 for the filming of both sequences, which fits neatly with Malins' description. While he was discussing his plans with the officer in charge of the heavy mortars there was a huge explosion, initially thought to be a mine. In fact one of Z29 Battery's 2-inch mortar pits had blown up. This event is recorded in the war diaries of 132 Howitzer Brigade and 29 Division Commander Royal Artillery, who attributed it to 'a faulty charge'. Corporal Haydn Price, Bombardier Frederick Howe and Gunner Harry Earp were all killed and their bodies were never recovered.[24]

With an officer as a guide, Malins and his assistant made their way through the shellfire to Lanwick Street:

> After clambering, crawling, running and jumping we reached a hole in the ground, into which the head and shoulders of a man were just disappearing . . . I looked down, and at a depth of about twelve feet was a trench mortar. The hole itself was, of course, boarded round with timber, and was about seven feet square. There was a gallery leading back under our parapet for the distance of about eighty feet and in this were stored the bombs. The men also sheltered there. I let myself down with my camera and threaded by the numerous 'plum puddings' lying there: I fixed my camera up and awaited the order for the men to commence firing. 'Are you ready?' came a voice from above. 'Right, sir,' replied the sergeant. I began to expose my film. 'Fire!' the T.M. officer shouted down. Fire they did, and the concussion nearly knocked me head over heels. I was quite unprepared for such a backblast.[25]

In 29 Division there were four medium batteries numbered S29, X29, Y29 and Z29, which had been formed in April 1916. The heavy battery, equipped with 9.45-inch pieces, was designated V29 and is seen in caption 23. Batteries normally comprised four mortars and some 5,000 rounds were fired during the bombardment. The personnel were from various infantry regiments although the heavy battery was crewed by the Royal Garrison Artillery. Each brigade also had a light trench mortar battery of 3-inch Stokes mortars, some of which can be seen in the sunken lane footage. The main objectives of the medium batteries were the cutting of wire and the

*The crew loading the 2-inch mortar in the cramped mortar pit.*
(IWM Q79486)

*A pit for a 2-inch mortar in Thiepval Wood, probably constructed in 1916 by men of the 36 Ulster Division. The base-plate was found in situ still pegged into a specially cut recess in the chalk at the bottom of the pit. The floor is at least thirteen feet below the 1916 ground level and the dimensions are comparable with the position filmed by Malins, although there is less evidence of timber shoring.*

destruction of enemy trenches, although the very limited range meant that the mortars were restricted to targets in the German front line.

While Malins was filming, the crew had problems with what he called the 'detonator', which was probably the blank .303 cartridge that fired the weapon. He was understandably nervous about being near a pile of ammunition after the fatal explosion earlier in the morning. In the film the mortar is fired twice with a cut in between which misses out much of the loading process and might be accounted for by the succession of misfires. One of the crew has a 29 Division battle patch on his tunic.

The viewing notes state that 'it has been claimed that this material might be faked and could have been taken at a trench mortar school; Malins is certainly linked to reports of fakery at such a location . . . Note the foot of someone apparently standing on the rim of the pit at the end of the scene, an unlikely position in genuine combat. If faked, it is at least well done – the scene is exciting and lacks obvious giveaways.'[26] It is far from being a fake, however, as all the evidence supports Malins' story. 1/2

Monmouthshire Regiment, the 29 Division pioneer battalion, dug mortar pits on Hawthorn Ridge. These were eight feet by eight feet square and thirteen feet deep with a dugout eight feet by five feet for the crew.[27] This corresponds very closely to Malins' measurements. The feet in the film are between five and six feet above the floor of the pit; for a six-foot tall man that would give at least a foot of head cover. He is not dangerously exposed and Malins describes the officer giving orders to the crew from above, so it is probable that the feet belong to the battery commander who can be seen to move away before the second round is fired. The mortar pit was probably near Lanwick Street to the north of White City.

**Date: 29 June 1916. Place: Hawthorn Ridge. Description: loading and firing a 9.45-inch trench mortar. Shots: 23.1–6. Stills: DH62–63. Cameraman: Malins.** The second sequence shows a 9.45-inch mortar being loaded and fired. This was a French design which the British used for want of anything better. The weapon with its base weighed nearly three and a half tons.

The dope sheet gives the date as 29 June, the location as White City and the battery as V21. The two former details are correct but on 29 June V21 Heavy Trench Mortar Battery was in front of Fricourt.[28] We suggest that the unit is in fact V29 HTMB, whose personnel were filmed on 1 July rescuing men from no-man's-land.

*Laying the piece was rudimentary and it was inaccurate. The elevation mechanism had a tendency to come loose and in the film the crew member in the foreground can be seen locking it in position by hitting it with a mallet.* (DH62)

**Date: 29 and 30 June 1916. Place: not located. Description: transport in a valley. General De Lisle addressing 2 Royal Fusiliers. Shots: 5.1–3. 10.3–4. Stills: DH19, Q726, Q728, Q737–738, Q748. Cameraman: Malins.**

The probable course of events, if the film caption is accurate, is that General Beauvoir de Lisle addressed 2 Royal Fusiliers on 29 June before the transport seen in shots 5.1–3 moved into the area. Shots 5.1–3 and 10.3 are of the same place. The situation is complicated by the fact that footage of two parades addressed by de Lisle has been edited together. The first battalion is said to be 2 Royal Fusiliers, shown with trees in the background. This is edited in with two shots of his address to 1 Lancashire Fusiliers, which is discussed below. De Lisle had taken command of 29 Division at Gallipoli in June 1915 and had been particularly impressed by the conduct of what he called his 'Fusilier Brigade' at Gully Ravine on 28 June. He had been keen to address both 2 Royal Fusiliers and 1 Lancashire Fusiliers on the anniversary but had postponed this because of the heavy rain. Perhaps encouraged by the improvement in the weather, he changed his mind and ordered parades for 29 June. Both de Lisle and the commander of VIII Corps, Lieutenant General Aylmer Hunter-Weston, used the example of Gallipoli to encourage their troops, although most battalions in 29 Division had few veterans of that campaign by June 1916. Malins quotes the text of de Lisle's speech and it is probably a fair reflection of what he said, with statements on the size of the Allied effort, the plight of the enemy and the need to uphold the traditions of Gallipoli.[29]

*General Beauvoir de Lisle in the unidentified valley talking to 'another general'; this officer appears in shots 10.3–4 and may be Brigadier General W.L. Williams who commanded 86 Brigade, although his face is not clear enough to make a comparison.*
(IWM Q728)

*The original caption reads: '1 Lancashire Fusiliers being addressed by their divisional commander, General de Lisle, before the battle of the Somme, Mailly-Maillet, 29 June 1916'. It is also reproduced in the* Lancashire Fusiliers Annual *for 1916 but the lack of back badges shows it is not that battalion and is probably 2 Royal Fusiliers.* (IWM Q738)

(Above and opposite page) *The film opens with the scenes shot in the valley, presumably on 30 June as the caption states, showing columns of horses, fatigue parties and a vast congregation of limbers and wagons. They represent the unglamorous but essential support units which formed over 30 per cent of the manpower of the army of the Great War.*
(IWM Q726, Q737, Q748)

**Date: 29 June 1916. Place: field next to the road junction on the southern outskirts of Mailly-Maillet. Description: General de Lisle addressing 1 Lancashire Fusiliers. Shots: 10.1–2. Cameraman: Malins.**

The back badges identify the men immediately in front of the camera as B Company, 1 Lancashire Fusiliers. The officer at the head of the company is probably Captain Cecil Wells, who appears in caption 35 shot at White City. The battalion commander, Lieutenant Colonel Meredith Magniac, must be in the film but the footage is not sharp enough to identify him. The second mounted officer is probably Captain Morres 'Bobby' Nickalls. He had been commissioned into the Northamptonshire Yeomanry in 1914 and was appointed aide-de-camp to General de Lisle on 11 June 1916. De Lisle had played polo with Nickalls before the war when he was at the Staff College and Nickalls was a student at Oxford. Nickalls was a barrister in civilian life and also a well known amateur jockey and a keen huntsman until his death in 1952.[30]

One eyewitness has left an account of this event. George Ashurst was a corporal in C Company, which was in fact in the front line on 29 June so how he attended the parade is something of a mystery. He was a Gallipoli veteran and, having a clear idea of the damage the schemes of generals could do to humble infantrymen, he was not very impressed by de Lisle's speech although he misidentified him as the Corps

*The site of General de Lisle's address to 1 Lancashire Fusiliers in 2007.*

commander. He also mentions that there was a lot of muttering in the ranks as de Lisle spoke. The text of de Lisle's speech survives in the Lancashire Fusiliers' war diary and the *Lancashire Fusiliers Annual* for 1916. While Malins was enthusiastic about such events, his driver David Laing would have agreed with Ashurst:

> One thing that amused and amazed me was the pep talks given by the brigade generals to the troops just before the big day of the Somme battles. They got the battalions to line up on a three-sided square, with the general addressing them on the enormous amount of troops and guns we had, and that Jerry's lines would be knocked into pulp. The British troops would then have nothing more to do than go over the top and walk right on to Berlin. But it was a different story on the first day when they went over after the bombardment lifted and were met by a fuselage [sic] of machine guns, etc. and were mowed down by the thousand and the roads were full of walking wounded, arms and shoulders, etc.[31]

**Date: 29 June 1916? Place: 'north of Albert'. Description: 4.7-inch gun being loaded and fired. Shots: 11.1–6. Stills: DH28, DH33, Q79483. Cameraman: Malins.**

The dope sheet indicates that this footage was shot on 29 June, which is possible. We cannot add much to the location 'north of Albert' as there are few clues in the film, although it is probable that Malins did not stray too far from Mailly-Maillet where we know he filmed General de Lisle on 29 June. By this period 4.7-inch guns were not common as they were being replaced by the more effective 60-pounders; there were only thirty-two of them on the Somme in June 1916 but unfortunately each Corps had at least one battery so trying to deduce a location through the documentary evidence is impossible. The 4.7-inch gun was principally used for counter-battery tasks which it performed with varying degrees of success. One noticeable feature of this footage is the very half-hearted camouflage and the lack of any protection for the gun.[32]

*A screen grab of the 4.7-inch gun being fired.*
(IWM Q79483)

## CHAPTER FIVE

# McDOWELL BEFORE
# 1 JULY 1916

John Benjamin McDowell has always been overshadowed by Geoffrey Malins in the story of filming the Battle of the Somme. He left virtually no record apart from inter-views which he gave to *Kinematograph and Lantern Weekly* on 10 July and to *Screen* on 7 October 1916. He apparently took no part in the editing of the footage and some material that he expected to see in the finished film did not appear. A common in-terpretation is that Malins alone was responsible for editing the film and is alleged to have deliberately selected his own footage at McDowell's expense. There is no explicit evidence that this is the case and equally no doubt that Charles Urban was in fact the editor. Urban may have had help from Malins but we suggest that he was quite capable of seeing through an attempt to favour one cameraman over another and would have judged the shots on their merits, regardless of who took them.

The best estimate is that the two cameramen shot about 4,000 feet each. Nicholas Hiley believes that 'the IWM print suggests that the final version of the film included only 25 per cent of the material McDowell took but a massive 82 per cent of the footage shot by Malins'. On the face of it this does support the case for Malins having favoured his own material but we believe that the balance is more even than Hiley indicates. We cannot confidently assign every single shot to one or other cameraman but each has about the same amount of footage in the film, based upon our analysis of the time and place of each shot, rather than taking the attributions from the dope sheet. If there is an imbalance this is as likely to be due to poor image quality, inaccurate record-keeping or mechanical failure as to deliberate manipulation.[1]

The first interview on Monday 10 July gives some insight into McDowell's working methods. He said:

I was under fire several times on the first day of the Big Push, and I am hopeful that I have secured a number of interesting pictures. No, the big gun fire and the concussion did not upset me, or interfere with my 'taking' as much as I had anticipated it might do. But I think this might have been due to the fact that years ago I was engaged on the proving of guns and ammunition at Woolwich Arsenal, and so became more or less familiarised with the reports of big gun fire.

In all, I have secured about 4,000 feet of negative, and some of the pictures, which, by the way, I am particularly anxious to see on the screen, should prove most interesting. I got a number of views in our front-line fire trenches – which were only 150 or 200 yards from the German line – and you can see our shells bursting. On the first day of the great offensive I secured pictures of the bombardment, of the prisoners coming in, wounded arriving, and a good general view of our troops in the open with the German shells bursting over them. The latter view naturally is in the distance, and I am curious to see how it turns out.[2]

Some of the shots he describes are clearly identifiable and are discussed below but there is no footage of troops advancing as he describes. Possibly the film was not sufficiently good to be included. There is one clue in a still photograph taken from the British front line at about the same place as shots 12.3–8. This is believed to have been taken by a cameraman from 1 Printing Company, Royal Engineers on 1 July although we have been unable to discover his identity or indeed if there was more than one. It does give an idea of what McDowell's footage might have looked like and may have been taken at the same time. The distant troops are possibly 1 South Staffordshire Regiment or 22 Manchesters from 91 Brigade, 7 Division.

There is contradictory evidence as to when McDowell departed for France. *The Times* states that he left on 28 June while *Kinematograph and Lantern Weekly* reported

*The 7 Division attack on 1 July taken by a cameraman of 1 Printing Company, Royal Engineers. (IWM Q89)*

that 'he had less than forty-eight hours in which to make the necessary arrangements before he left for France, and four days after his arrival "The Big Push" began'.[3] Brooks Wilkinson asserted that he set out 'within a few hours after leaving the meeting'. He would have acquired a camera, a supply of film and a uniform before leaving. He presumably did not know the date on which the offensive was due to start so he had the additional concern of trying to get there before it was launched. McDowell remembered:

> I would not have missed it for anything. At the same time I've seen a good deal I'm never likely to forget. Things move so rapidly at the front, however, that one's first impressions soon become blurred. Strange to say, I was more worried and nervous during my journey from Charing Cross to Dover about the success of the pictures I hoped to take, than ever I was in the trenches with the German bullets whizzing overhead.[4]

McDowell described the difficulties of filming: 'I walked through miles and miles of trenches, and you may guess it was no easy job getting along with a heavy camera and tripod, often through deep mud and slush. On the day after the great advance we "borrowed" a German prisoner and he carried the camera for us, which made things a bit easier.' In his October interview he elaborated:

> Naturally from the firing line back five miles the land is alive with shell-bursts and a cinematograph operator's life there, getting to the front with his apparatus, is not enviable. The camera weighs about forty lbs to begin with, but after carrying it along roads and over broken country with the 'crumps' going off casually and then along the trenches for hours, it seems to weigh about four

*McDowell and his camera in the trenches. The small box respirator worn by the man on the left dates the photo to after July 1916.* (Kevin Brownlow)

hundredweight. We start out under the guidance of a captain whose name deserves to be better known and no doubt will be some day, and our car takes us as near the scene as it is considered safe for a car. Then we get out and look for trouble. One gets smothered with dirt thrown up by bursting shells. It even gets into the mouth.

Sadly we have no clues as to the identity of his conducting officer. McDowell's experience gave him a great respect for the resilience and humour of the British Tommy: 'It never ceases to astonish you. The more you see of them the more you wonder at them and admire them. They make grim jests at fate. Nothing daunts them.'[5]

We give below the shots taken by McDowell before 1 July but as we have little information on his movements we cannot be sure if the order is entirely accurate.

**Date: 27–29 June 1916? Place: probably around Meaulte. Interior and exterior of a covered gun position containing a 60-pounder gun. Shots: 13.1–3. Stills: DH39, IWM FLM 1651. Cameraman: McDowell?**
The dope sheet gives the date of this shot as 27 June and the place as 'Albert Road' – a very unhelpful description. Shot 4 of this caption was filmed near the Sucrerie facing Beaumont Hamel and is discussed in chapter 4. The significant clue to the first three shots is the mention of a Canadian battery. Only three Canadian batteries that served on the Somme in June 1916 have been traced and the best candidate is 1 Canadian Heavy Battery which used 60-pounders from February 1915. The Corps boundary with III Corps ran from the Ancre just north of Meaulte to Bécourt. No detailed maps of battery positions in this area are known and there is little in the footage to suggest a location. Unfortunately the battery war diary gives no map reference for its position before 1 July. The attribution to Malins is doubtful as this is a long distance from the area in which he took all his footage. If the battery is indeed Canadian, this footage may have been taken by McDowell although it is not certain that he had arrived in France on 27 June so the date would be incorrect. The suggested location around Meaulte or even further south would certainly favour McDowell.[6]

**28 June 1916? Place: north of Bray-sur-Somme. Description: French women working in a field. Shot: 7.1. Still: DH20. Cameraman: McDowell.**
This shot is attributed by the dope sheet to Malins near Albert but was actually filmed from west of the D147 road from Bray-sur-Somme to Fricourt.

**Date: 29 June 1916? Place: railway line south of Bécordel. Description: 6-inch howitzers firing on Mametz. Shots: 12.1–2. Stills: DH32, DH35. Cameraman: McDowell.**
The scene is shot from the railway embankment running towards Bécordel. It consists of a pan of a single howitzer, followed by a static shot of four howitzers firing. The Willow stream can be seen in the background as can the ruined village of Bécordel.

*The gun position is well constructed with earth side walls reinforced with timber. There is a burster layer of sandbags laid on corrugated iron sheeting. Although more elaborate than other gun pits seen in the film the position seems genuine; the layout conforms to plans of covered positions for the 60-pounder.*

*A tent with a red cross on it can be seen in the distance, presumably part of an ADS or MDS. The site of Bray Hill cemetery is visible in this shot but it was only established in 1918. (DH20)*

The access road from the D938 runs down the hill and takes a left turn before crossing the Willow stream. To the right of the road is a stand of trees concealing a section of the embankment of the old metre-gauge railway line from Albert to Peronne, on which McDowell placed his camera. The dope sheet seems to allocate these shots to 29 June, which would fit with McDowell's arrival in the area. No location or cameraman is given.

The guns in this sequence are 6-inch 30cwt breech-loading howitzers, from one of three batteries allocated to XV Corps before 1 July. The appendices to the XV Corps artillery war diaries are missing and it is impossible to identify the individual battery. The 30cwt howitzer was obsolescent by 1914 and was not an entirely successful design, being very short-ranged for its size. From 1915 onwards it was replaced by the 6-inch 26cwt howitzer which could fire twice as far. It is very surprising that the gun position has no protection at all. The shells are piled up next to the pieces which are entirely out in the open with no concern for German counter-battery fire. The bagged charges seem to be stored in the lee of the railway embankment or perhaps in a brick-lined culvert that still exists.[7]

*The railway embankment runs towards Bécordel village and then takes a left turn before the stream. Only one 6-inch howitzer is visible in this shot.* (DH32)

*The tree growth on the old railway embankment makes an exact comparison shot impossible. The Willow Stream runs along the trees at the foot of the slope with the southern end of the village visible in the distance.*

**Date: 29 or 30 June 1916. Place: east of Mansel Copse. Description: the bombardment of Mametz. Shots: 12.3–8. Still: DH39. Cameraman: McDowell.**

The six shots that follow the footage of the howitzers show shells landing on the German trenches in front of Mametz and on the village itself. The viewing notes cast doubt both on the location and the genuineness of the footage. The film was in fact taken from the British front line above the present-day coach parking bays in front of Mansel Copse.

This footage is of historical significance as it shows part of the terrain over which 2 Gordon Highlanders and 9 Devonshire Regiment passed on the morning of 1 July. It is very much the scene that Captain Duncan Martin of 9 Devonshire Regiment looked on with such trepidation. The story is well known and is recounted in Martin Middlebrook's *The first day on the Somme* as well as being mentioned in the *British Official History*. While on leave Martin constructed a plasticine model of the area and deduced that his men were vulnerable to fire from a German machine gun in the village cemetery. His prophecy came horribly true and he died with many of his men on the slope above Mansel Copse. He is buried in Devonshire Trench Cemetery.[8]

In shot 12.4 the Albert to Peronne road can be made out. The narrow gauge railway ran parallel to it on the north side. 2 Gordon Highlanders jumped off from the trenches in the film attacking along the valley towards the railway station.[9]

*The position from which McDowell filmed the shelling of Mametz. The view is looking north-west towards the village on the horizon with the D938 in the foreground. McDowell filmed shots 37.1–3 from the bank in the middle distance. The German front line is just beyond the left-hand end of the bank.*

*The top two views show shells landing on the enemy's support line. Hidden in the smoke are the village cemetery and the shrine with the machine gun post. The third photograph shows the British front line and the fourth image is of the British support line with the German trenches beyond.* (DH39)

**Date: 28–30 June 1916. Place: Bois des Tailles. Description: men of 2 Royal Warwickshire Regiment in bivouacs. Shots: 18.1–6. Stills: DH55, DH56, Q79488. Cameraman: McDowell.**

Caption 18 is dated by the dope sheet to 29 June 1916, which adds that 'this regiment moved off into the firing line the same evening'. The viewing notes suggest that the troops are 2 Royal Warwickshire Regiment of 22 Brigade, 7 Division. This battalion was in 'tents and hutments' in the Bois des Tailles between Morlancourt and Bray, having arrived there on 25 June. They were due to move on the evening of 28 June but the postponement of the attack delayed their departure until 10.50pm on 30 June. McDowell could have filmed them at any time between 28 and 30 June. If the caption is correct, the most likely date would be the evening of 30 June. A number of men

*A panorama from* Sir Douglas Haig's great push *which has been stitched together from individual frames from the film for inclusion in the book. The man with the white armband in front of the bell tent on the right of the second photograph is also seen behind the bivouac with his hand to his mouth, apparently filling a pipe. In the film he walks from left to right and therefore appears twice. The man in the cardigan (second from left), wearing a cap comforter, appears in shot 18.3 walking across the screen from right to left, thus providing a link between shots 18.1 and 18.2–3. A number of the panorama sequences in the book were very skilfully assembled in this fashion although close examination shows some joins.* (DH55)

appear in more than one shot, thus linking them all together, and it is quite possible that McDowell took them within minutes of each other.[10]

The first shot comprises a long pan from left to right over the bivouac area showing an assortment of improvised shelters, some bell tents in the background, and men sitting about. One man, seen in the second photograph below, has a white band on his right lower sleeve which indicates he is a wire cutter according to the scheme of badges set out in 7 Division orders.[11] The same man appears again in shots 18.5 and 18.6, thus proving the footage is of the same unit. No other battalions of the Royal Warwickshire Regiment served in XV Corps, which supports the identification of the men as being from the second battalion. The man on the far left of the pan is putting on his equipment which is the 1914 leather pattern, a type not normally issued to regular battalions. The wood was packed with troops and it is probable that he was from a different unit.

Shots 18.2 and 18.3 show the distribution of stew into mess tins. The scenes are framed by two temporary timber huts and the background of sparse woodland seems to fit with the previous shot. The presence of 'a white grenade two and a half inches in length on right sleeve just below the shoulder' confirms that the men are from 7 Division. It was worn by men detailed as bombers rather than those who had qualified for the trade badge.[12]

Shot 18.4 is unconnected. Taken in July 1916, it shows a group of men in goatskin jerkins. This footage is very similar to a scene in part 2 of *The Battle of the Ancre and the Advance of the Tanks*, which the dope sheet to that film dates to 4 November 1916.

*Screen grab from shot 18.2 showing bomber's badges on the men on the left-hand side.*

*Shots 18.5 and 18.6 show a group of men eating round a fire. 18.5 is a long shot with a left pan while 18.6 shows the centre of the group. This photograph is a screen grab from shot 18.6. One man on the left has a Royal Warwickshire Regiment cap badge. The man to the right and behind the soldier with the steel helmet putting his spoon into his mess tin appears in shot 18.1. The viewing notes mention the peculiar hairstyle of two men on the right and one at the back with close-cropped hair and a long tuft at the front which is said to be 'somewhat in vogue in the army of 1916'.[13] (IWM Q79488)*

**Date: 30 June 1916. Place: Bray-sur-Somme. Description: 7 Buffs listening to orders; troops marching through Bray-sur-Somme. Shots: 6.1–3. Stills: DH20, Q79478. Cameraman: McDowell.**

Bray-sur-Somme is about 5 miles south-east of Albert and had been a British billeting and headquarters area since the summer of 1915. Because it was near the boundary between the British and French armies it was often used also by French troops who can be seen in one shot. The dope sheet attributes this footage to Malins, but he was at White City on 30 June.

Shot 6.2 is of a column marching up the main street in Bray-sur-Somme. The men are wearing 1914 pattern equipment and are loaded with bandoliers and PH hoods. There is an illegible symbol on the helmet covers. In addition a flag and two heart-shaped markers on short poles are being carried. The viewing notes offer 8 Suffolk Regiment, 18 Division as possible subjects, probably on the basis that their name

*Shot 6.1 shows a parade in a side street in Bray-sur-Somme. The viewing notes identify the battalion as 7 Buffs (East Kent Regiment) of 18 Division on the basis of the letter 'B' visible on the officer's helmet cover and the fact that they are mentioned in the caption. It might equally well stand for 'Bedfords' who appear in shot 6.3 and have a device, possibly a letter 'B', on their helmet covers. Alternatively the letter may merely show the officer's company. The men wear helmet covers without any insignia on them and also 1908 pattern equipment which is unusual, although not impossible, for a New Army battalion.*
(DH20)

*The same street in 2007.*

appears in the caption and that the Buffs and Bedfords are accounted for in shots 6.1 and 6.3.

Shot 6.3 shows D Company, 7 Bedfordshire Regiment, 18 Division. This identification is given in Martin Middlebrook's *The first day on the Somme* where the officer is named as Lieutenant Douglas Keep, although the origin of this information is not known. Comparison with a photograph of Keep shows that they are the same man. The battalion arrived in Bray from the trenches at 1am on the morning of 29 June and spent the day resting. They moved back up for the assault sometime during 30 June and were filmed by McDowell who had set up his camera in the main street.[14]

The equipment worn by the men conforms exactly to paragraph 20 of the battalion operations order issued on 30 June 1916, which lists 'Equipment to be carried on the men. Every man will carry: – Rifle and equipment less pack. One bandolier in addition to his equipment ammunition (170 rounds in all). One day's ration and one iron ration. One waterproof sheet, two sandbags, one yellow patch on haversack on his back. Two smoke helmets. Grenadiers will only carry fifty rounds SAA.' According to the 18 Division operations order of 23 June the yellow patch on the small pack was the divisional identification although no example appears in the film. 7 Bedfords was a New Army battalion and the men are wearing 1914 pattern equipment. The 'smoke' or PH helmets in their cases are slung one over each shoulder, while the waterproof sheet and the sandbags seem to be folded on top of the haversacks on the back; the cotton ammunition bandoliers can also be seen. They are not excessively loaded down although the orders state that 50 per cent of them would have to pick up additional tools at a dump nearer the front line.[15]

Douglas Scrivenor Howard Keep was born in Sydney, New South Wales on 17 June 1893, the second son of John Howard Keep and Agnes Rosa Keep. Douglas had an elder brother, Leslie, who also served in 7 Bedfords. The family must have returned to Britain as Douglas was educated at Leighton Park School in Reading and later went to Wadham College, Oxford, where he was a member of the Officer Training Corps for two years and rowed for his college. He enlisted in the Public Schools Battalion of the Middlesex Regiment on 11 September 1914 at St James Street, London, while simultaneously applying for a commission in the Bedfordshire Regiment. He and his brother Leslie were medically examined at the same time and both men stood six foot tall. Douglas was commissioned as a temporary second lieutenant in the Bedfordshire Regiment on 29 September 1914. Leslie Keep served in the same battalion and survived the war. Promoted to lieutenant in the spring of 1915, Douglas went overseas with 7 Bedfords on 26 July 1915.

On 1 July D Company was in support of the two assaulting companies and suffered a number of officer casualties although Keep escaped unscathed. The battalion was involved in the assault on Thiepval village in September and he was awarded the MC for his part. He was promoted to acting captain with effect from 28 October 1916. On

*A grab of a platoon of D Company, 7 Bedfordshire Regiment marching north out of Bray-sur-Somme on 30 June 1916 with Lieutenant Douglas Keep at their head.*
(IWM Q79478)

*The same street in 2007.*

*A photograph of Douglas Keep taken from* War Illustrated, *18 August 1917.*

15 July 1917, at the age of 24, he was killed by a shell while supervising a working party near the banks of Zillebeeke Lake south of Ypres. He was buried at Reningholst New Military Cemetery.[16]

**Date: 30 June 1916? Place: Bray-sur-Somme or Morlancourt? Description: column of troops marching right to left past camera. Shots: 6.4–5. Stills: DH21, Q79479–79481. Cameraman: McDowell.**

The final two shots of caption 6 offer a fascinating glimpse of a British Army battalion on the march, showing rifle companies, Lewis gun sections and transport. Unfortunately we have been unable to identify either the battalion or the place. The dope sheet attributes the whole of caption 6 to Malins. The other shots in the caption were undoubtedly taken in Bray-sur-Somme and can be dated fairly securely to 30 June 1916, a time at which McDowell was in the area. There is no certainty that this material has any relationship with the previous scenes. A search of Bray-sur-Somme failed to produce anywhere that resembled the scenery in the shot and we would welcome any suggestions.

The viewing notes suggest that the men are from 1 Royal Welsh Fusiliers, on the basis that the Buffs, Bedfords and Suffolks are seen in the other shots. However, the entire battalion is wearing 1914 pattern equipment, which was almost exclusively issued to New Army battalions and would not have been worn by a regular battalion. The troops are wearing steel helmets but there are a few in service caps; the cap badges, although not clear enough to identify, do not resemble those of the Royal Welsh Fusiliers.

*The unidentified battalion on the march headed by Lewis gunners with their carts and a man leading the company commander's horse. The 1914 pattern leather equipment is clearly visible on the men behind.* (IWM Q79479–79480)

**Date: 28 June 1916. Place: Bois des Tailles. Description: Manchesters' church parade. Shot: 14.4. Stills: DH44, Q79485. Cameraman: McDowell.**
The shot comprises a left pan over a church parade with a hillside in the background. The viewing notes point out that a sergeant at the end of the shot has the crossed pick and rifle of a pioneer battalion on his collar and suggests that the men are from 24 Manchester Regiment, the pioneer battalion of 7 Division. Other men appear to be wearing collar dogs but they are not readable. The dope sheet gives the date of 28 June which probably means that McDowell filmed this shot shortly after his arrival and that it may have been taken around the Bois des Tailles, which is where the 24 Manchesters and 2 Royal Warwickshires were located on that day. There is no mention of a church parade in the 24 Manchesters war diary but the men were resting on 28 June so might have been able to attend one. McDowell remembered 'I was present, and got a picture of an open air church service, attended by the troops before going into action', which confirms the dope sheet attribution to him.[17]

**Date: 28–30 June 1916. Place: not located. Description: a battalion of the Royal Warwickshire Regiment marching along a road. Shot: 21.1. Stills: DH57, DH58, IWM FLM 1658. Cameraman: McDowell.**
This shot shows a battalion on the march along a road with a barn-like building in the distance. The dope sheet gives McDowell as the cameraman and states that it was shot

*Church parade in the valley of the Bois des Tailles.* (IWM Q79485)

'near Albert' on 29 June. The viewing notes provide the additional location of the 'Bécourt–Bécordel road', although it is not certain where this information comes from. The terrain in the film does not match that between Bécourt and Bécordel and the actual location is probably some distance away from the trenches. The viewing notes suggest the battalion is 2 Royal Warwickshire Regiment but, like the column seen at Bray in shot 6.3, these men wear 1914 pattern equipment and are therefore unlikely to be regulars. None of the men seen in caption 18, which we can securely identify as 2 Royal Warwickshire Regiment, is wearing shorts. A photograph on p. 58 of *Sir Douglas Haig's great push* is captioned 'a new battalion of the Royal Warwickshire Regiment resting on their way to the trenches' and shows men in shorts sitting beside the road. This is a grab from missing film which is still extant in a compilation entitled *The Holmes Lecture Film* (IWM Film and Video Archive 468/2). Nothing is known of Holmes but the five reels were put together from *The Battle of the Somme* and other films sometime after 1918. A grab from the existing footage is on p. 57 and states that 'reserves were being marched up to the reserve trenches over the greater part of the British lines previous to July 1'. Unless the dope sheet is wrong in every respect and the men shown are from 48 Division, which had several battalions of Warwickshires,

*A shot showing part of the battalion on the march. Note the shorts and the badges on the front of the helmets.* (DH58)

*The screen grab of the excised footage.* (DH57)

we suggest that the film shows men of the 10 Royal Warwickshire Regiment, who spent the days preceding 1 July in the Morlancourt area in III Corps reserve and at least are 'new' and 'reserves'.[18]

**Date: 28–30 June 1916. Place: Minden Post? Description: Royal Artilleryman holding fox cub. Shot: 7.6. Still: DH24. Cameraman: McDowell.**
The dope sheet gives the date of this shot as between 25 and 30 June 1916, although it is probably nearer the latter. The scene is credited, probably correctly, to McDowell. The gunner holds a very tame fox cub. Soldiers of the Royal Artillery, RAMC and Queen's Regiment can be seen. 2 Queen's Regiment was part of 91 Brigade, 7 Division. The dugouts visible in the background may be part of the shelters constructed in the south side of the road embankment at Minden Post. McDowell took about six and a half minutes of film in this location but there is not enough detail to make a conclusive identification.

We have no indication of where McDowell spent the night of 30 June 1916 but his filming on 1 July and after is described in Chapter 8.

## CHAPTER SIX

# MALINS ON 30 JUNE 1916

Either by accident or design Malins missed Friday 30 June 1916 from his account. We believe it is likely that a number of scenes were filmed on this day, some of which were described as having been shot on 1 July. All this footage was shot within a few hundred yards of the front line and shows men who went over the top the next morning.

**Date: 30 June 1916. Description: Men of 1 East Lancashire Regiment, 16 Middlesex Regiment and Seaforth Highlanders at White City. Shot: 28.1. Stills: DH70, Q796. Cameraman: Malins.**

This footage shows men in full equipment outside a dugout. The accompanying still, Q796, is captioned '16 Middlesex Regiment (29 Division) parading for the attack on Beaumont Hamel, July 1916', which would seem a clear enough identification. It also demonstrates that Malins and Brooks worked together, as some individuals appear in both the still and moving images taken here. Although the staff sergeant on the right has Middlesex shoulder titles, virtually all the cap badges resemble that of the East Lancashire Regiment. Probably the most persuasive evidence is in Paul Reed's *Walking the Somme*, in which he states that the men are from 1 East Lancs and identifies the officer in Q796 with his back to the camera removing his cap as Second Lieutenant Norman Frank Currall. Currall's photograph album survives in private hands and a copy of Q796 is annotated by Currall himself. Norman Currall was killed in action on 18 October 1916 while serving with 1 East Lancs and has no known grave.[1] The battalions of 4 Division wore sacking covers on their helmets with a scheme of coloured badges. 16 Middlesex belonged to 29 Division which did not have helmet covers. Photographs of 16 Middlesex show them wearing 1914 pattern equipment while these troops are wearing 1908 pattern. In the background of both images is a party of 2 Seaforth Highlanders with the 'C' badge in white cloth on their arms. This seems to be peculiar to their carriers and does not, as is often said, stand for Seaforth. Confusingly the 1930s part work *Twenty years after* has a photograph showing an unnamed veteran of 16 Middlesex at White City in 1936 in the same spot as Q796. He is quite high up the bank and may be one of the men on the right-hand side of the photo who could be Middlesex.[2] Noel Peters, who served in 16 Middlesex on 1 July 1916, claimed to recognise a number of men in the photograph and suggested that it was taken before the battle.[3] With such contradictory views it is difficult to know what

*The upper photograph is Q796 and the lower is a screen grab. Note the number of men in both shots. The head and shoulders of the Middlesex staff sergeant are visible in the screen grab at lower right. The soldier at the bottom of the steps has a cloth 'C' on his left arm. (IWM Q796, DH70)*

to believe but we suggest that Currall's photograph album is the crucial piece of evidence and that the majority of the men in Q796 and the film are from 1 East Lancashire Regiment, with a staff sergeant from 16 Middlesex and a number of 2 Seaforth Highlanders in the background.

**Date: 30 June 1916. Description: C Company, 1 Lancashire Fusiliers at the junction of Tenderloin and King Street, White City. Shots: 28.2–4. Stills: DH71, Q744, Q79490–79491. Cameraman: Malins.**
Critical evidence for this familiar material comes from stills, in particular Q744 taken

by Brooks from the parapet above the trench. The man on Brooks' left is Malins, who is getting down into the trench to take a sequence of three shots showing the men fixing bayonets and moving up King Street trench towards the firing line. The third sequence shows a captain supervising more men including bomb carriers as they also turn into the trench and disappear out of shot to the left. The place is the area behind the British front line north of the Beaumont Hamel to Auchonvillers road. Being in the lee of an escarpment running north to south gave the position some shelter from hostile artillery and there were numerous dugouts built into the bank. Because of the chalk spoil the area was known as White City after the stadium in West London.

The back badges and the painted hackles on their helmets identify these men as C Company, 1 Lancashire Fusiliers. C Company and the party designated to be left out of the attack occupied the front line in the days leading up to the attack. The company commander's orders stated: 'the company will move from Mailly Wood to White City on the afternoon before the bombardment commences, moving via

*This photograph is looking south with Hawthorn Ridge in the background. 2 Royal Fusiliers attacked from Marlborough Trench which runs diagonally across the hillside. It appears in the footage of the assault on 1 July seen in shots 31.3–4 as well as that of the rescue of a wounded soldier from no-man's-land in shot 34.1. Corporal Holland is on the left of the shot, CSM Nelson on the right and an unidentified second lieutenant in the centre. (IWM Q744)*

*Screen grabs from caption 28 showing the same scene from Malins' position.*
(IWM Q79490–749491)

*The same area in 2006.*

Auchonvillers and Third Avenue by half platoons at 200 yard distance. During the bombardment they will live in the dugouts at Tenderloin where the two sections of Monmouths will join them before the attack.'[4] The date of this footage is probably 30 June 1916; in his memoirs Corporal George Ashurst of C Company remembered being called out to be photographed before 1 July in exchange for 'a tot of rum and a packet of cigarettes'.[5] Unfortunately Ashurst is not recognisable in the extant footage. Two men in this sequence were identified at the time in the *Lancashire Fusiliers Annual*, for 1916. The NCO on the left of the shot is Corporal Holland, who survived the war. Company Sergeant-Major Edward Nelson is on the right.[6] Nelson was commissioned into the King's West African Rifles after recovering from wounds received on 1 July. The fact that Nelson and his company commander, Captain Edmund Dawson, were both wounded immediately they went over the top proves that the footage was shot earlier; this is confirmed by the empty trenches, which Ashurst recalled were crowded on the morning of 1 July. The men are wearing 1908 webbing with the small pack and many of them have the famous tin triangles attached. They carry the usual assortment of smoke helmets, rolled ground sheets and bandoliers of ammunition and do not seem overloaded.

The officer in the centre of shot is wearing an other ranks' tunic with a set of 1908 pattern equipment. The battalion operation order stated: 'officers will wear men's clothing and equipment with badges of rank on the shoulder. Sticks will not be carried.' This may not have been strictly adhered to as the machine gunners of 119 RIR who destroyed the Lancashire Fusiliers' attack the next morning reported that the officers were identifiable at the head of their men. Some were even said to be carrying swords.[7] We believed that this officer might be Second Lieutenant William Caseby but comparison of a photograph with a screen grab by Professor Alf Linney, a facial recognition expert, showed that they were not the same man. The only other candidate is Second Lieutenant Ernest Sheppard, who appears in a photograph of 10 Manchester Regiment before the war but the image is not good enough to make a conclusive match.[8]

We encountered better luck with the officer in shot 28.4. This shot continues from the previous one and shows a taller, thinner man wearing captain's insignia on his shoulder straps. He is also wearing a private's tunic with 1908 equipment and a large pack with a tin triangle hanging from it. This officer could be Captain Edmund Dawson, who commanded C Company on 1 July 1916. The Fusiliers Museum in Bury supplied a photograph of him which Professor Alf Linney matched to a screen grab. The comparison is achieved using two photographs of the face taken from the same angle and scaling them so that they are the same size. A number of measurements of the face remain constant during life, such as the distance between the base of the nose and the top of the upper lip. These can be compared and if a sufficient number match in the two photographs there is a good chance that they are of the same person or of two people who look very alike. In this instance we only had one candidate whose measurements matched the face in the film.

Edmund McNaghten Dawson was born in Southbourne in Hampshire on 27 September 1889 and was educated at Haileybury. After Sandhurst he was gazetted to 2 Lancashire Fusiliers at Tidworth but went out to India in 1910 to serve with 1 Battalion. Dawson played rugby, squash and tennis and was a competent boxer and horseman. 'Pongo' Dawson, as he was known, was home on leave in August 1914 and was posted to 9 (Service) Battalion on its formation in Bury. He became Brigade Machine Gun Officer in October. Promoted to captain in 1915, he landed at Gallipoli on 7 August, whereupon he became temporary major commanding 5 Lancashire Fusiliers. He was wounded in November and after a short spell with 3 (Reserve) Battalion he rejoined 1 Lancashire Fusiliers in France. Badly wounded at 7.30am on 1 July 1916 he spent several months in hospital before returning to France to command W Company of 9 (Service) Battalion. He was wounded yet again in an attack south of Langemarck on 16 August 1917. A contemporary remarked 'nothing much deterred Pongo' and he was out in France again in 1918. He remained in the army at the end of the war, served in India again before commanding the regimental depot and finally becoming second in command of 1 Battalion. He retired in 1934 and died suddenly in Oxford on 1 January 1964. His obituary described him as 'an excellent regimental officer who took part wholeheartedly in all the activities of the battalions which he

*Edmund Dawson as a young second lieutenant with 1 Lancashire Fusiliers in India in 1911.* (Fusiliers Museum, Bury)

*A grab from shot 35.1, with Edmund Dawson in the centre.* (IWM Q65410)

served with'.[9] During the making of the Channel 5 documentary *The Battle of the Somme: The True Story* Edmund Dawson's grand-daughter Anne Dawson was traced and she was able to see her grandfather on film, not as the elderly gentleman she remembered but as a young officer in the middle of one of history's greatest battles. This scene shows Dawson watching the men of his company as they turn up King Street towards the front line. C Company was to be the consolidation company and a number of men can be seen with boxes of grenades slung between poles precisely as required in Dawson's operations order:

> All men not carrying wiring materials will carry boxes of bombs which will be dumped in the German first trench. These bombs will be found in stores in our trenches and in Tenderloin and will be carried by two men carrying three boxes slung on the wooden pickets for wiring. When the boxes are dumped these pickets will be taken on. The boxes will be ready slung on poles on the evening prior to the assault.[10]

**Date: 30 June 1916. Description: Men of C Company, 1 Lancashire Fusiliers with engineer stores at White City. Shot: 29.1. Stills: DH77, Q731. Cameraman: Malins.**

*A grab very similar to Q731 which is captioned 'wiring party of the Royal Warwickshire Regiment going up to the trenches; Beaumont Hamel, July 1916.' Both Q731 and shot 29.1 in fact show C Company and were probably taken shortly after caption 28. The first four men past the camera appear as the last four men in the previous shot and the soldier standing in centre shot is CSM Nelson with Corporal Holland behind him. The unidentified officer can also be seen walking away from the camera. The distinctive sandbagged dugout in the background was north of the junction of King Street and Tenderloin and appears in Q734. After going up King Street in the previous shot the men turned left on to the berm where there was a dump of engineer stores. The men picked up rolls of wire, bundles of silent pickets and wooden mauls for knocking in the pickets.[11] (DH77)*

**Date: 30 June 1916. Description: two wounded men at King Street, White City. Shot: 35.1. Stills: DH90, Q65410, Q101064. Cameraman: Malins.**
Because of the presence of Captain Edmund Dawson in this shot we can say for certain that it was not taken on 1 July as Dawson was wounded shortly after 7.30am on that day. Some time has certainly elapsed between this shot and the previous ones as Dawson is now wearing an officer's service dress jacket. He has 1908 pattern equipment but without the large pack. Two casualties appear, the first in a fireman's lift and the other on a stretcher. The British trenches were being shelled throughout this period so there is no reason to believe the casualties have been faked for the camera.

Malins described the atmosphere after dark as the trenches filled with men and preparations went ahead for the attack. He did get some sleep despite the noise and the cold but was woken by a Lancashire Fusiliers officer as daybreak came.

*The RAMC medical officer in the foreground directs the casualties to his left, which would eventually take them to the 87 Field Ambulance ADS at the Red Barn in Auchonvillers. He is wearing a private's tunic and has his stethoscope round his neck. He is unidentified but we believe he is the Regimental Medical Officer (RMO) of 1 Lancashire Fusiliers; the other medical officer in the area was Captain Clark of 87 Field Ambulance who was in charge of the Tenderloin dressing station but he had been wounded by shellfire in the neck and chin a few days before. Although he remained on duty, his injuries would almost certainly have been visible.[12] (IWM Q65410, Q101064)*

# CHAPTER SEVEN

# MALINS ON 1 JULY 1916

According to his own account Malins was woken at dawn on 1 July 1916 by the noise of gunfire. He was told by an officer that he could film in the sunken lane in no-man's-land which had been occupied by B and D Companies of 1 Lancashire Fusiliers. A tunnel known as Sap 7 had been driven out from the British front line although this did not, as is often thought, go all the way to the sunken lane. It emerged in no-man's-land and was continued by a four foot deep trench dug the previous evening by 1/2 Monmouthshire Regiment. Malins and his guide forced their way through the crowded tunnel and along the sap. As the latter was visible from the German lines it had to be negotiated with care.

**Date: 1 July 1916. Description: men of B Company, 1 Lancashire Fusiliers and no. 1 Section, 86 Trench Mortar Battery in the sunken lane in front of Beaumont Hamel. Shots: 32.1–5. Stills: DH82, IWM FLM 1672–1673. Cameraman: Malins.**
Malins took nearly a minute of film here at some time before 6.30am when he returned to the front line along Sap 7. B Company was up against the east bank of the road nearest the enemy to avoid being seen. D Company was further up the lane where it was shallower and provided less cover. The caption states that the position came under fire shortly afterwards although it was from 77mm shells rather than machine guns. The first shot is looking south and shows Fusiliers and some men of 86 TMB, with one of four 3-inch Stokes mortars. The mortars and ammunition were carried along the cramped Sap 7 while Malins was also trying to get through. Visible on the left is a runner with his armband, and chalk spoil from the sap can be seen on the right. Malins then moved the camera a few yards down the lane and filmed the mortar men and the runner from the opposite direction. About fifty minutes after Malins left, the mortars began a bombardment of the German front line and at 7.30am the men of B and D Companies climbed out of the sunken lane and advanced across no-man's-land. After a few seconds they were hit by machine-gun fire and the men either went to ground or managed to crawl back into the lane.[1]

Malins forced his way back down the tunnel. He claims to have filmed men fixing bayonets although we believe that if this is the surviving footage from caption 28 it

*The third shot was filmed from further down the lane and shows a second lieutenant with his back to the camera. He is having a conversation with the man facing him, who is saying 'I hope we are in the right place this time, because if not I am going to bomb them all and get out of here.' (DH82)*

*Authors Fraser and Roberts in the sunken lane at about the point where Malins filmed.*

was almost certainly shot the previous day. He was alarmed that his previously reconnoitred position at Jacob's Ladder had been badly damaged by shelling and he had to move the camera back. He got himself ready to film the mine explosion on the opposite side of the valley. At thirty seconds after 7.19am he began turning and watched his film dial with concern as the film exposed. Finally the earth began to tremble.

**Date: 1 July 1916. Place: White City. Description: mine exploding under Hawthorn Ridge, Beaumont Hamel, filmed from White City. Shots: 29.2–3. Stills: DH75, Q22, Q754, Q756, Q50324–50325. Cameraman: Malins.**
Malins' footage is about twenty-three seconds long with a slight pause as the cloud of dust expands. It is possible that he stopped momentarily to conserve film. The mine was constructed by 252 Tunnelling Company, Royal Engineers and was intended to destroy the Hawthorn Redoubt or Weissdornfeste, which had a good field of fire over the valley leading down towards Beaumont Hamel. Despite the Germans having prior knowledge of the attack from telephone intercepts, the explosion of the mine was a complete surprise. However, casualties were light as it exploded under the tip of the position rather than in the centre. An entire platoon of 9/119 RIR was entombed but many men were able to dig themselves out, some not getting free for several hours. The Germans organised counter-attacks almost immediately. Two platoons of Z Company, 2 Royal Fusiliers with machine guns and trench mortars had been given the task of taking the crater but failed to gain a foothold.[2]

The camera position has been a source of some dispute but we have now been able to fix it within a few yards. We surveyed the trenches from 1916 maps and marked them on the ground with mine tape. An important feature no longer in the landscape was a line of trees at the bottom of the valley; these appear in the footage of the mine explosion and were taped out. By aligning them and other terrain features with screen grabs we got an accurate position for the camera on the top of the escarpment back from Jacob's Ladder. Brooks took at least two photographs very close to Malins. When looking at the screen grabs it is not at all apparent that the land drops away sharply beyond the sandbagged trench in the middle distance.

*Brooks' photographs of the mine explosion. Note the tops of the trees to the left which appear on trench maps and enabled us to fix the camera position on the top of the escarpment at White City. The archaeologist and aerial photography pioneer O.G.S. Crawford took photographs of the mine from an unrecorded location in the reserve trenches and described seeing 'men and bits of planking' being lifted into the air but nothing of that nature can be seen here. Unfortunately Crawford's photographs were not usable 'because the plates were stale'.[3]* (IWM Q754 and Q756)

*Photograph of the Hawthorn mine taken by an unknown cameraman. It is possible that this is one of O.G.S. Crawford's shots that did come out. (IWM Q22)*

*The position from which Malins filmed the Hawthorn Redoubt mine. Probably because of the lens he was using, the image in the film looks as if it was shot from somewhat further away than it actually was.*

*View through a loophole in Marlborough Trench on the south slope of the valley, with a comparison view taken in 2007. The German lines are in the distance and small-arms fire from there probably accounted for the men seen to fall in shot 31.3. The buildings on the skyline mark where the heavy shells landed in caption 20. This section of trench is the refuge of the two men recovering the casualty from no-man's-land in shot 34.1. The photograph was taken on 26 July 1915 when the British relieved the French in this sector.* (IWM Q50324)

*The view in July 1915 from Jacob's Ladder looking across the valley to Marlborough Trench and the area filmed in shots 31.3 and 34.1. (IWM Q50325)*

**Date: 1 July 1916. Place: White City. Description: British soldiers crossing no-man's-land from Marlborough Trench to the Hawthorn Redoubt mine crater, filmed from White City. Shots: 31.3–4. Stills: Q745, Q750, Q755, Q757. Cameraman: Malins.**

As the earth subsided Malins swung his camera round and filmed troops going over the top. The first two shots of caption 31 were taken at Ligny-St-Flochel and are discussed in Chapter 10. Shots three and four are genuine but the identity of the troops is unlikely to be resolved. The dope sheet states 'Middlesex and Royal Irish advancing in the distance. Royal Fusiliers and Lancs.' If Malins is correct in his comment that he began filming 'the engineers swarming over the top and streaming along the skyline', the troops in shot 31.3 are probably from the two platoons of Z Company, 2 Royal Fusiliers who were to seize the crater prior to the main attack. The only men visible are on or just below the skyline and heading directly towards the crater. Had Malins filmed the main attack there would probably be more men in the shot. A file of six men can be seen leaving Marlborough Trench and moving across no-man's-land before turning down towards the road. The leading two men fall just before the footage ends abruptly. The behaviour of this isolated file of men was curious and so we decided to retrace their progress using members of No–Man's–Land. Six men ran from the taped-out trace of Marlborough Trench towards the old German line until they reached the point at which their predecessors had turned left. On leaving the trench they were in dead ground and relatively immune from small-arms fire to their front. To take advantage of this shelter they kept left but became visible to the Germans in the trenches on the north side of the valley and the first two men were hit by fire from there. This may be the point at which Malins changed his film magazine. We only have Malins' account to go by, but he seems to have filmed at least the beginning of the main attack on the same reel as the first sequence. When the camera begins running again there is a large body of men moving towards the German lines.

*The view from Malins' camera position over the north slope of Hawthorn Ridge. This photograph demonstrates the mundane nature of combat when filmed from a distance.*
(IWM Q750)

We have no indication of how long Malins stopped his camera if he was changing film. A practised cameraman could remove and replace a magazine in about one minute. The large body of men that appear in shot 31.4 could be other members of Z Company or part of the main assault which jumped off at 7.30am. Malins must have taken several minutes of film from this position, of which about fifty-nine seconds appears in the film. It is unclear what the relationship is between the two surviving portions. The first wave of attackers within the camera's field of view consisted of 1 Lancashire Fusiliers and 2 Royal Fusiliers. This is at least consistent with the dope sheet description. The second-line battalions in this area were 1 Royal Dublin Fusiliers on the right and 16 Middlesex on the left but, because the trenches were blocked with wounded, these troops did not get over the parapet until 7.55am. These men probably equate to the 'Middlesex and Royal Irish' described in the dope sheet. Whether Malins stayed in the same position long enough to film these battalions is unknown. The history of 16 Middlesex describes Malins as the man 'who photographed the 16 Middlesex going over the top on 1 July 1916', although we do not know if this is accurate. Brooks certainly stayed there as he took Q755 which shows men withdrawing to the British lines.

*It is probable that Q755 was shot at about 10am when the Royal Fusiliers and Middlesex around the crater abandoned the position despite the efforts of Lt Col. Hall of 16 Middlesex to rally them. Peter Barton suggests that a figure seen by the road bank waving a cane above his head may be Hall. Alternatively the photo could have been taken about noon when the 2 Royal Fusiliers' war diary records that 'the few remaining men in no-man's-land were forced to retire', but by this time both Brooks and Malins were probably in the Tenderloin area.*[4] *(IWM Q755)*

*Marlborough Trench and the trees by the Old Beaumont Road in 1916 and 2007. It is not clear what the soldiers were doing in the British wire.* (IWM Q745)

**Date: 1 July 1916. Place: Tenderloin, White City. Description: wounded man being rescued from no-man's-land and carried towards Tenderloin collecting post (CP). Casualty being evacuated on stretcher. Shots: 34.1–3. Stills: DH86, DH89, Q752–753, Q79501. Cameraman: Malins.**

Malins and Brooks seem to have made their way to Tenderloin, which was full of wounded men, and walked down to near the New Beaumont Road. The thirty seconds of caption 34 and a still photograph follow the rescue of a man from no-man's-land to his arrival at the collecting post, involving at least five men. Shot 34.1 was filmed from near the New Beaumont Road and features two soldiers carrying a wounded man. The man on the right in this footage appears to be wearing a cardigan. Malins reports that the Germans were turning machine guns on would-be rescuers. According to him a trench mortar man had asked for a volunteer and the two had gone out to tend to a man crying for help. Between them they got him into Marlborough Trench.

Malins was present as the casualty was transferred from 'cardigan man', who was one of the rescuers out in no-man's-land, to 'shirt sleeve man'. As 'shirt sleeve man'

*Q753 was taken by Ernest Brooks who was positioned at the junction of Marlborough Street trench and the New Beaumont Road. In the image a man in a cardigan carries a casualty on his back across the road, moving in the direction of the dressing station at Tenderloin. For some reason this trench did not go under the road and the rescuer had to cross in full view of the enemy. Malins had nearly come to grief here when he used this trench in the opposite direction to get on to Hawthorn Ridge on 29 June. (IWM Q753)*

*Brooks then turned half left and took this photograph of two men crawling on hands and knees towards the trench. They are on the New Beaumont Road and are probably Lancashire Fusiliers who were wounded earlier.* (IWM Q752)

*The same place in 2007.*

*Shot 31.2 continues with a man in shirt sleeves moving towards the camera carrying a man on his back. The casualty is the same man earlier photographed by Ernest Brooks. He appears to be unconscious and although badly injured, has no obvious wounds. The left sleeve and side of his tunic are torn and there are also tears to the right sleeve. On his upper sleeve is a 29 Division battle patch. (IWM Q79501)*

moves along the trench, over his right shoulder can be seen an exhausted 'cardigan man' leaning against the wall of the trench. Strangely he has been handed what looks like a tin of corned beef. As 'shirt sleeve man' moves past the camera he is followed by a lance corporal who also appears in shot 31.3.

The identity of the two rescuers has eluded researchers for decades and sadly they are likely to remain anonymous. The Imperial War Museum has correspondence relating to over fifty individuals who have been suggested as one or other of the rescuers; some accounts even suggest that the footage was faked. In our investigation we have seen photographs of two candidates who resemble 'shirt sleeve man'. When the photograph of one man was put to Professor Linney he detected a good match but research revealed that this soldier did not go to France until February 1917. The other man was with a battalion of 29 Division, was in the area on 1 July 1916 and also looks very like 'shirt sleeve man'. However, we cannot be sure exactly what he was doing on that day; the rescuers were fairly certainly from a trench mortar battery and there is no evidence that the man had any involvement with this weapon.

It appears that Malins repositioned his camera further north and a short time later resumed filming nearer Tenderloin. In shot 31.3 two men are seen carrying a casualty on a stretcher, moving towards the camera. There are no SB armbands or RAMC badges visible. Both are wearing steel helmets and display the single stripe of a lance corporal or lance bombardier on their upper sleeves. Neither man appears to be carrying any form of gas helmet. The man on the stretcher is the casualty seen in the previous shot. The presence of carriers from the Seaforth Highlanders with the cloth 'C' on their sleeves fixes the location as the White City area. The casualty is said by the caption to have died thirty minutes later while Malins says he survived for twenty minutes. The caption of Q753 claims that he is from 1 Bedfords, but that unit was not in the battle area on 1 July. It is possible that this is an error for 1 Border Regiment, which went over the top not far away.

Born in Tilbury, Essex in 1894, Walter Henry Lydamore was employed as a seaman by the Port of London Authority and enlisted in the Royal Garrison Artillery at Gravesend on 27 August 1914. He served with 47 and 461 Siege Batteries and on 21 April 1916 he was promoted to lance bombardier. On 21 May 1916 he was posted to V29 Heavy Trench Mortar Battery. Lydamore said: 'I remember seeing the camera crew there. We were bringing wounded in from no-man's-land but had to stop because of enemy machine-gun fire.' His memories back up Malins' account and confirm that members of V29 HTMB were used to assist the RAMC and regimental stretcher-bearers, who were overwhelmed by the casualties. It is some satisfaction that one of these gallant men now has an identity.[5]

*The lance corporal leading the stretcher was previously seen behind 'shirt sleeve man' in shot 34.2. He is no. 46379 Lance Bombardier Walter Henry Lydamore, V29 Heavy Trench Mortar Battery, Royal Garrison Artillery. Walter Lydamore of Leigh-on-Sea in Essex recognised himself in this piece of film in a documentary about Sir Winston Churchill. An article on the story appeared in the* Southend Pictorial *of 23 December 1964.*

**Date: 1 July 1916. Description: walking wounded of 1 Lancashire Fusiliers around the entrance to the Tenderloin CP, White City. Shots: 35.5–7. Stills: DH91, DH105, Q739, Q65413–65414. Cameraman: Malins.**

The first shot was taken around the area seen in the previous footage looking north along Tenderloin towards the entrance to the collecting post. Several of the wounded seen here appear in the next shot, including the runner in shorts and the man in the right foreground with his left tunic sleeve slit. Many of the men have had their wounds dressed but only the runner has an Army Form 3118. This recorded a man's identity and treatment and was normally fixed to his clothing at the RAP if he had been treated there by the RMO.

Shot 35.6 begins with six of the casualties from the previous shot walking past the camera. They are presumably on their way back up Third Avenue to the 87 Field Ambulance ADS in Auchonvillers. Behind them an RAMC private is helping the man seen in Q739. They are making slow and painful progress up the trench with the casualty exclaiming 'Jesus, Jesus'. The two men arrive at the entrance to the collecting post and an officer with a bandaged head sitting in the entrance rather reluctantly makes

*Wounded waiting for evacuation at Tenderloin. The man on the right is the casualty with the wound to his foot seen in shot 35.6. (IWM 739)*

*Captain Cecil Wells (centre) smoking a cigarette.* (IWM Q65414)

room for the casualty to get past. The officer, clearly groggy, moves to the other side of the trench.

The medic beckons to someone behind the camera and says 'Sarge, Sarge. This man needs a carry.' Two more wounded men come past the camera with AF3118 forms attached to their tunics; one has shaken hands with another man in the background before moving towards the camera. The wounded officer is Captain Cecil Francis Wells, who commanded B Company in the sunken lane on the morning of 1 July 1916. On going over the top 'the leading two lines of B and D Companies had a few moments grace and then the enemy MG opened and a storm of bullets met the attack. The third and fourth lines of B and D Companies were practically wiped out within a few yards of Sunken Road, only some wounded, including Captains Nunneley and Wells, the two company commanders, managed to crawl back.' Wells remained with his men for another six hours before he was forced to retire to Tenderloin. As he was wounded

*Captain Cecil F. Wells, probably in 1917.*

shortly after 7.30am this would put the time of the filming at about 1.30pm or later. He probably came back from the sunken lane through Sap 7 with other wounded men. Second Lieutenant Sheppard had also been wounded and timed the evacuation at shortly after 1.00pm. Both Wells and Sheppard were awarded the MC for their bravery that day.[6]

Cecil Francis Wells was born on 21 July 1883 in Sotwell, Berkshire and was first commissioned as a second lieutenant in the Army Service Corps (TF) but resigned his commission in 1912. Rejoining in 1914 he went to France in March 1915 and served with 2 Lancashire Fusiliers in the Ypres Salient. He was slightly wounded on the right cheek in April and was gassed and evacuated to England in May. Cecil Wells returned to France and joined 1 Lancashire Fusiliers. On 1 July he received a gunshot wound to the face and was hit in the hand. He commanded a battalion in December 1917 and was wounded a fourth time in 1918. Wells remained in Berkshire after the war and seems to have suffered no serious effects from his wounds as he was a noted tennis player in the 1920s. He and his wife Sarah had a son, Alfred Francis Wells, who was born in 1907. He was commissioned in the Berkshire Regiment and was killed in action on 31 May 1940. He is buried in Houthulst churchyard, near where his father had served in the previous war. In 1948 Cecil Wells commissioned a memorial window to Alfred in the church at Rotherfield Peppard in Berkshire.[7]

**Date: 1 July 1916. Description: troops resting at White City. Shots: 56.1–2, 56.4. Stills: DH151, Q730. Cameraman: Malins.**
Malins remained at White City until 2 July. Shot 56.1 is usually thought to show 1 Lancashire Fusiliers but we suggest that it is 2 Lancashire Fusiliers, 4 Division. The men wear helmet covers which are not seen in the footage of 1 Battalion and there are

no 29 Division battle patches. The queue of men in trousers on the far right of this shot wear on their arms the 'C' badge, which was not unique to the Seaforth Highlanders.

Shot 56.2 is linked to Q730 which is captioned as showing the Royal Warwickshire Regiment. The terrain matches the top end of White City and the troops are 2 Royal Warwicks, 4 Division which had come forward from the sunken road after 9am that morning. What appears to be a Royal Warwickshire cap badge is visible on one of the men in this shot. This battalion was not heavily engaged on 1 July and lost only fifteen men killed.[8]

Shot 56.4 was also taken at the north end of White City and shows odd groups of soldiers with no semblance of order. Given the proximity of the front line, it is curious that nobody seems to be concerned about possible enemy artillery or mortar fire.

*This photograph was taken some fifty yards further south and on the other side of the shallow ditch in which the men are sitting. In the distance the ciné camera, fairly certainly a Moy and Bastie, can be seen on its tripod beyond the dixie of water which appears in shot 56.2. Malins was presumably in the process of filming shot 56.2 as Brooks took this photograph. The trench railway in the background appears in Q746 and can be seen in action in shot 56.5. (IWM Q730)*

*The general area of Q730 and shot 56.2.*

**Date: 1 July 1916. Place: White City. Description: carrying parties of 2 Seaforth Highlanders assembled for roll call. Shots: 56.5, 58.2–4. Stills: DH153, Q746. Cameraman: Malins.**

Malins took four shots of the roll call, which happened sometime in the afternoon, and described the scene: 'in one little space there were just two thin lines – all that was left of a glorious regiment (barely one hundred men). The sergeant stood there with a note-book resting on the end of his rifle, repeatedly putting his pencil through names that were missing.' However, the carrying parties under Captain McPherson had been deployed to White City and were there all day; the battalion itself was in the German lines around the Quadrilateral until after dark when the survivors made their way back and assembled in the sunken road north of Auchonvillers during the night. They remained there on 2 July and were joined by the carriers. This would suggest that the men in the photograph are not the remnants of a once-proud battalion but in fact the fortunate hundred or so who did not go over the top that morning.[9]

*Brooks' shot of the roll call taken from the bank of White City with the railway in the background. Malins took shot 56.5 from very much the same place and the figure next to the sergeant may be Malins himself.* (IWM Q746)

*The roll call of 1 Lancashire Fusiliers. Malins filmed shots 28.2–4 from the roof of the shelter on the right and the dugout in the background is that seen in shot 29.1.*

**Date: 1 July 1916. Description: men of 10 Brigade MGC cleaning machine guns at White City. Shots: 59.1–2. Still: DH154. Cameraman: Malins.**

The dope sheet identifies these men as '10 Machine Gun Corps' but incorrectly dates the photograph to 9 July 1916. The unit identification and place are correct, however. 10 Brigade Machine Gun Company arrived at Tenderloin on the evening of 30 June. Eight guns accompanied the attacking battalions of 10 Brigade and four remained in reserve at Tenderloin. By the end of the day the survivors were back in the British front line where seven guns were deployed. The remaining five guns were sent back to Tenderloin. Allowing for sixteen guns in the company and four of those being lost, there should have been five guns at Tenderloin – which is exactly the number seen in shots 59.1–2.[10]

*10 Brigade MGC on the afternoon of 1 July.* (DH154)

CHAPTER EIGHT

# McDOWELL ON 1 JULY 1916 AND AFTER

## Minden Post

The footage shot at Minden Post is probably the earliest material shot by McDowell on 1 July 1916. It has never received the attention that it deserves compared to that taken by Malins around White City. Some six and a half minutes of film survives, showing British wounded and prisoners returning from the front line and the treatment of the casualties of both sides. Minden Post lies on the south side of the embankment of the main Albert to Peronne road as it crosses a shallow valley which runs down the west side of Caftet Wood. In 1916 a brick culvert, visible in several shots, ran under the embankment; this has been buried by road improvements in the last twenty years.[1] In June 1916 the site was used by units of 7 Division.

There is confusion in the attribution of some Minden Post footage. The dope sheet states that Malins was responsible for captions 42 and 43, the latter being incorrectly numbered caption 34. Some authors have accepted the dope sheet and believe that Malins filmed here but there is strong evidence that all this film was shot by McDowell on 1 July when we know Malins was at White City.

**Date: 1 July 1916. Place: Minden Post, south of Caftet Wood. Description: a pan over Minden Post, looking north-west, followed by a shot of walking wounded. Shots: 40.1–2. Stills: DH112, DH113, Q65417, Q65418. Cameraman: McDowell.**
The dope sheet gives the date of the footage as 2 July 1916 but it is more likely to be 1 July. Shot 40.1 is a left pan across Minden Post.

The shot begins by showing a number of men with bicycles, probably from XV Corps Cyclist Battalion, who are wearing full infantry equipment with light-coloured squares of cloth attached to their small packs. One man without equipment has a square of material sewn on the back of his tunic. The 7 Division operations order stated: 'a square patch of pink flannel will be sewn on the flap of the haversack, – the top edge level with the seam marking the turnover of the flap. This will allow the patch

*Parts of the pan across Minden Post.* (IWM Q65417–65418)

to hang loose with the bottom level with the bottom of the haversack when full.' This unusual arrangement is useful for identifying footage shot in the 7 Division area,[2] and has remained unnoticed for ninety years, unlike the tin triangles used by VIII Corps.

As the camera pans round you can see the dugouts built into the embankment as well as the dressing station for the lightly wounded set up by the culvert and the large sandbagged signal office. In the foreground are three German medics, two of whom are wounded. They are identifiable in shot 34[43].2. These men and at least four other unwounded prisoners are wandering freely. Caption 44 refers to 'Manchester Pioneers waiting to go down to the German trenches when captured', probably 24 Manchester Regiment which was the 7 Division pioneer battalion. As their war diary for July 1916 does not survive we cannot confirm this identification.

The second shot of the caption is a close-up of three British soldiers with head wounds. They have been treated at the walking wounded dressing station and three men with bandaged heads can be seen coming from this direction in shot 40.1, although it is not certain if McDowell has moved the camera in to get close-ups of them or if they are different men. The dugouts behind and out of shot to the right are those used as the 22 Field Ambulance ADS and it is possible the men are going there to be documented as none of them has Army Form W3118. The kilted bomber with no obvious wounds is from 2 Gordons and an officer of the same regiment can be seen on the right talking to two other kilted soldiers.

**Date: 1 July 1916. Place: on the main Albert to Peronne road above Minden Post. Description: loading an ambulance on the main road; treatment of wounded further down the road. Shots: 41.1–4. Stills: DH117, Q65419, Q65420, Q79504. Cameraman: McDowell.**

The first shot is on the main Albert to Peronne road, now the D938. The dope sheet has 2 July 1916, although 1 July may be correct. The medical personnel are from 22 Field Ambulance, which was responsible for the ADS at Minden Post. A report written by the commanding officer on 7 July 1916 stated that at this period and up to 8am on 2 July 'there was a great scarcity of motor ambulances coming to Minden Post, only five cars reaching there during this time. The cars had now begun to run right up the Peronne–Albert Road above Minden Post. From 8am onwards the supply of cars was good and by midnight the battlefield was cleared of wounded.'[3] An RAMC captain can be seen looking at a casualty on a stretcher. 22 Field Ambulance had five officers at the Minden Post position but it is not possible to identify this captain. At the end of the shot two French soldiers walk past the camera.

Shot 41.2 shows the outside holding area for stretcher cases awaiting evacuation from the ADS. This was constructed by 22 Field Ambulance and involved the excavation of an area of the eastern slope of the valley. The chalk spoil from this operation can be seen at the end of shot 40.1, although there is no sign of it today. Seven stretcher cases are visible and many of the RAMC personnel are in shirt sleeves, which shows it is already warm. It is likely that the footage was shot in the late morning of 1 July

*Men of 22 Field Ambulance prepare to load an ambulance. Note the stretcher-bearer in the left-hand shot using sandbags as padding for his shoulders. The man with the red cross armband in the centre of the right-hand shot is an RAMC captain. (DH117)*

*The same place on the D938 in 2007.*

before large numbers of lying cases began to arrive. The main communication trench to the rear was Norfolk Avenue, which became blocked by reinforcements and was impassable to the Furber wheeled stretcher carriers which meant that the bearers had to carry the casualties down to the Divisional Collecting Station at Vauxhall. The commanding officer's report states that 'by 2pm the congestion at Minden Post became great . . . but was temporarily relieved by the employment of 200 prisoners of war who were made to carry stretchers to Vauxhall'. The report continues: 'at this period there was a dearth of stretchers (I indented for fifty stretchers at 10.30pm from CCS) and received 25 at 4.30am the following morning'. A rolled-up stretcher in the shot suggests that it was filmed before they became scarce. The build-up of untreated casualties became more serious later in the day because 'at 12 midnight there were 125 stretcher cases at Minden Post and the trench from here to the culvert was blocked with cases'. The statistics in the 22 Field Ambulance war diary show that up to 9am

*The area outside the 22 Field Ambulance ADS. The man on the stretcher on the left-hand side is protecting his head from the sun with his steel helmet. He has an AF W3118 attached to his tunic, one of only two men in the entire Minden Post footage who has one. The caption gives the date of this shot as 1 July 1916, which we believe to be correct, rather than 2 July as shown on the dope sheet.*

*A general shot of Minden Post from the south in 2007 showing the area of the ADS on the right. The culvert and the walking wounded dressing station are to the left of the water trough.*

*A scene from shot 41. In the background is a more seriously wounded casualty on a stretcher; he is removed by bearers in shot 41.4. The soldier with the bandaged head in the centre background has a pickelhaube as well as his own steel helmet.* (IWM Q65420)

on 2 July 5 British officers and 196 men of 7 Division were treated, in addition to 6 other ranks of other divisions and a German officer and 12 other ranks. These figures do not include the lightly wounded, however. Up to 9am on 5 July 1916 the unit treated and evacuated 6 officers and 246 other ranks, both British and German. Contrast this with 87 Field Ambulance of 29 Division, whose men appear in the White City footage: by noon on 3 July they had treated 2,111 casualties, an appalling contrast between the human cost of a failed attack and a successful one.[4]

Shots 41.3 and 41.4 were taken close to each other as the same casualty on a stretcher appears in both shots. Although undoubtedly at Minden Post, these shots cannot be linked to any others. In the back of shot 41.3. is an entrance to an underground shelter. It is possible that McDowell went through the culvert to film on the other side of the embankment in Caftet Wood. The pile of equipment and rifles against the bank are likely to have been discarded by walking wounded. The first shot shows an RAMC sergeant partly removing the dressing from a wound to the foot of a stretcher case. He is surrounded by a crowd of interested spectators obviously attracted by the camera. The RAMC stretcher-bearer at the end of the shot is an eloquent portrait of stress and exhaustion as he puffs on a cigarette.

**Date: 1 July 1916. Place: Minden Post. Description: treatment of walking wounded by 22 Field Ambulance, RAMC. Shots: 44.1–7. Stills: DH118–120, Q65435, Q65439, Q65440, Q79514. Cameraman: McDowell.**
The other sequence of wounded at Minden Post is caption 44. It is composed of seven pieces of film showing the treatment of lightly wounded men at the dressing station beside the culvert. The report states that 'at Minden Post the cases were separated, the walking cases being seen and if necessary dressed at a small dressing station set apart for this purpose. They were then directed to walk down Norfolk Avenue to Vauxhall to the Divisional Collecting Station.' The dressing station was a small open-sided shelter with little protection against shellfire. It had a bench along the back with a spirit stove and a stock of dressings. A sandbagged wall ran out from it and curved round to provide some protection and sitting space for casualties waiting for treatment.

In shot 44.1 about eleven wounded men appear, some walking past after examination and others sitting on logs by the sandbag wall awaiting treatment. Some men are checked by two shirt-sleeved medical orderlies, both of whom appear in later shots. Again there is a crowd of interested onlookers from the battalion in the background; two of the spectators appear to have Manchester Regiment cap badges which would reinforce the identification of the troops as 24 Manchester Regiment. Shot 44.2 pans right towards the dressing station catching two surprisingly cheerful soldiers with head wounds whose attention is drawn by the curly-haired man sitting in front of the camera. The buttons on his collar indicate he is a German non-commissioned officer. Also visible in the background is a man in a steel helmet wearing a sleeveless cardigan or jumper, engaged in assessing casualties. He has what looks like an RAMC badge on his helmet cover and is possibly a medical officer, although he has no rank badges visible. The camera pans back to the left in shot 42.3 catching a small man with a chest wound. He is wearing the liner from a helmet on his head; these became detached accidentally or deliberately and were often worn as makeshift hats in the 1916–1918 period. One of the orderlies brings forward a casualty who is naked from the waist upwards. The camera follows this man into the dressing station. In the next four shots we see him having his wounds treated. He has been extremely lucky to have clean 'through and through' wounds to both upper arms. He has a full range of movement in his arms and does not appear to be in severe pain; he is given that staple of the Great War medical treatment regime, a cigarette, and is able to put it behind his ear for later. The wounds to the left arm have bled but there is little visible blood loss from the right arm. It is possible that they were inflicted by the same projectile if he had both arms raised but we cannot be certain of the cause; it was probably a low-velocity object such as a pistol bullet or a shrapnel ball. A rifle round or shell fragment would have caused considerable tissue damage. The orderly, whose trousers are torn, revealing his under-

*The soldier with the wounded arms during treatment at the walking wounded dressing station, showing the bleeding from the left arm.* (IWM Q65439)

pants, applies iodine with a brush, a painful process that the casualty accepts without flinching.

**Date: 1 July 1916. Place: Minden Post. Description: wounded and prisoners walking past the camera. Shots: 42.1–3 and 34\*.2–5 (\*misnumbered and should be shot 43). Stills: DH120, Q65434–65435, Q79506–79508, Q79511–79513. Cameraman: McDowell.**

The final segments of the Minden Post footage comprise captions 42 and 43, the latter incorrectly numbered 34 in the film. These are shot from two positions, the first being in the centre of Minden Post facing north-west, which is about fifty-five seconds long, and the second by the prisoner holding area on the lane at the back of Minden Post which is forty-eight seconds of film. Caption 42 ends with German prisoners on the edge of the lane. This location also features in shot 43.1 before the scene returns to Minden Post in shots 34[43].2–5. It is probable that the film was shot in one operation at each location and edited later, rather than that McDowell moved his camera about more than was necessary.

The Minden Post scenes are crowded and full of action, from which it is worth extracting a few interesting points rather than describing the whole in detail.

*Screen grab from shot 42.1 showing a wounded soldier.* (IWM Q79506)

*A wounded and dazed soldier (shown in shot 42.3) being led towards the ADS.*
(IWM Q79508)

Shot 42.2 shows the first batch of prisoners arriving. The war diary of 14 Brigade Royal Horse Artillery states that 7 Division captured 23 officers and 1,359 men.[5] McDowell filmed German prisoners at Minden Post, on the road south of there and about a mile to the north on the slopes to the west of Carnoy. The last will be discussed in due course, as we suggest that it was filmed later in the day. Men of 109 RIR can be seen both at Minden Post and near Carnoy, but no German soldier appears in more than one location and these are separate batches of prisoners. The men seen here were probably on their way to the rear or carrying stretchers by the time McDowell was filming near Carnoy. 109 RIR suffered very heavily on 1 July with 100 dead and 264 wounded. In all, 2 battalion commanders, 9 company commanders, 4 medical officers and no fewer than 1,750 other ranks were listed as missing, although many of these were believed to be dead.[6]

The 7 Division operations order of 17 June 1916 set out the provision for prisoners: 'A Divisional Prisoner Collecting Station will be established at a point 200 yards south of Orchard Camp . . . As a rule 5 per cent of the number of prisoners will be a sufficient escort. Officer prisoners should be kept separate from the men. Care should be taken that documents in possession of prisoners are not thrown away on their way back.'[7] Shot 42.2 shows twenty-two prisoners in various uniforms. Most men in this footage had shoulder straps with their unit number on but the film quality is not adequate to read more than a few. By July 1916 infantrymen generally could be wearing one of three patterns of tunic, the pre-war Waffenrock with full cuff and piping detail, the transitional tunic sometimes wrongly described as the M1910/15 or 1914 pattern, or the economy pattern Bluse with fly front. Examples of all three appear in the film. Most men in shot 42.2 wear the Waffenrock with Brandenburg cuffs having three vertical buttons. Three men are from 109 RIR, which is discussed below. The last man in the line is a curiosity. He is dressed in well-tailored M1915 Bluse, trousers and boots, and has officer's shoulder straps; his neat appearance is rather let down by his headgear which looks like a pair of underpants. He is smoking a cigarette and talking in a relaxed fashion to the British lieutenant of either the Royal Artillery or Royal Engineers behind him. This officer makes a friendly remark to him as they part company. Further back is a well-dressed major from either the Royal Artillery or the Royal Engineers. He exchanges words with the lieutenant, the major saying, 'I am terribly sorry. I did not realise you were waiting for me.' Shot 34[43].4 shows two groups of sixteen and fifteen prisoners with guards. Most of these men wear the Waffenrock with Brandenburg cuffs, a few have Swedish cuffs and three have the intermediate pattern tunic. Two of the first and one of the second group are from 109 RIR.

Shot 34[43].5 displays a total of thirty-seven prisoners. They mostly wear the Waffenrock, with a few in the intermediate pattern. Four men have Swedish cuffs and the remainder Brandenburg cuffs. Two medics are noticeable, one with a head wound. These men appear in the wide pan of shot 40.1 implying that McDowell moved his camera shortly afterwards to take that shot. One of the escorts has a German Pickelhaube front plate attached to his helmet cover. This was a popular practice and there are other examples in the film. The wearing of regimental badges on the helmet or its cover is prevalent here as well as in 29 Division.

Many of the prisoners shown in the film are without headgear. Soldiers in shots 36.1 and 47.1 can be seen carrying pickelhauben that they have acquired. Archaeological evidence of 'souveniring' has been found by No-Man's-Land in the excavations at Ultimo crater on the southern end of the Messines battlefield of June 1917. An Australian soldier was recovered in August 2008 with a large pack containing bully beef tins and a Hessian pickelhaube. The Stahlhelm was not in common use on the Somme in July 1916 and 109 RIR was probably not issued with them until October 1916. Few have their equipment and gas masks and only one NCO in shot 34[43].5 has retained a bread bag and water bottle.

The viewing notes suggest that the men are from the Grenadier Battalion of '109th (Württemberg) Reserve Infantry Regiment'. 109 RIR was in fact part of 28 Reserve Division, which was from Baden. According to the regimental history, the first and second battalions were issued with the same uniform as their regular counterparts, 1 Badisches Leib-Grenadier-Regiment, except that the shoulder straps bore the number 109 instead of a crown monogram. This was an unusual distinction for a reserve regiment, further complicated by the fact that the third battalion had fusilier lace on the collar. In shot 42.2 three men are wearing the Waffenrock with the distinc-

*A well-known incident from shot 34[43].5 in which a wounded British soldier barges a German prisoner who has accidentally knocked into him. This is the only sign of hostility towards prisoners in the film. Note the staff officer on the left-hand side of the shot who appears frequently. (IWM Q79513)*

*A few men have been allowed to keep their greatcoats and some use them to shade themselves from the sun. (IWM Q65435)*

*A studio portrait of a private soldier of 109 RIR. He is wearing the M1910 Waffenrock tunic and has a helmet cover on his pickelhaube. Note the collar lace showing that he is from the third battalion.* (Ralph Whitehead)

tive cuff and collar detail of III/109 RIR. Those without the collar lace are probably from I/109 RIR.

109 RIR had been on the Somme since September 1914. In common with most regiments they had had a fairly quiet time for the previous year. The last days of June were very different, however, and on the night of 30 June a relief was attempted; such was the weight of British shellfire that this had to be abandoned after Lieutenant of the Reserve Bobislawsky and 4 Company of 23 IR had replaced 4 Company of 109 RIR south-east of Mametz. The only other troops to get forward were four sections of 1 Company with their commander, Lieutenant of the Reserve Preuss, who relieved a few men of 12 Company, 109 RIR. The remainder of 23 IR got no further forward than Montauban.

The other prisoners are probably from the small portion of 23 IR who reached the front line. The regiment certainly wore the Brandenburg cuffs as seen on these prisoners and some men may have the figure 23 on their shoulder straps. The regimental boundary with 62 IR ran west of the Carnoy to Montauban road and therefore was in the 18 Division area. Prisoners from this regiment would probably have been removed from the battlefield further to the east. 23 IR was part of 24 Infantry Brigade, 12 Infantry Division, a Prussian regular formation. Infanterie-Regiment von Winterfeldt (2. Oberschlesisches) nr 23 had been raised in 1813 and was recruited in Silesia, although one concern in all the division's regiments was the number of ethnic Poles who were considered not loyal to Germany. Despite this perceived handicap, 23 IR had been through some hard fighting and was rated as a good regiment in a good division at this point in its history.[8]

**Date: 1 July 1916. Place: track running south of Minden Post. Description: giving water and cigarettes to prisoners. Handing back documents to prisoners. Shots: 42.4–5, 34[43].1. Stills: DH121, Q65436–65437, Q79509–79510. Cameraman: McDowell.**
This footage comprises three similar shots of a party of Germans sitting by the roadside with a group of interested British infantry and guards watching proceedings.

In shot 42.4 a young soldier with a Queen's cap badge appears among the escort, and therefore some of the prisoners may be from the recently arrived 1/23 IR who were in the area overrun by 2 Queen's.[9] This soldier is also seen in front of the signal office at Minden Post in shot 34[43].3 indicating that much of this footage was shot about the same time. On the left of the shot is a major with a coloured band round his steel helmet. This officer is also visible in other shots and in shot 34[43].5 he can be seen with a bundle of paybooks. The significance of the band on the helmet is unknown, although it is likely that he is a divisional or brigade staff officer. The next shot begins with a British officer giving a German casualty a drink from a water bottle, seemingly at McDowell's prompting. Another soldier comes forward, again probably encouraged by the cameraman, and offers cigarettes, as do several other men just before the end of the shot.

*A grab from shot 34[43].1. Some of the prisoners are having their papers examined, probably the* Soldbuch *or pay book that every soldier carried. This contained details of enlistment, training, pay and the units with which an individual had served. Analysis of the contents could give useful information on the enemy's order of battle and manpower situation. German*

*soldiers frequently carried diaries, letters and postcards and the chance survival of such paperwork has enabled No-Man's-Land to identify German soldiers killed in the Hohenzollern Redoubt and at Serre. (IWM Q65436)*

*The group of prisoners and their escort on the road at the back of Minden Post. Note the young soldier of 2 Queen's Regiment who also appears in shots 34[43].2–3.*
(IWM Q79509)

*Shot 45.2 was achieved by turning the camera a few degrees to the right and shows the British trenches on the ridge further east also under heavy shellfire.* (IWM Q79515)

*The same view in 2007. Traffic travels very fast on this road and care should be taken.*

**Date: 1 July 1916. Place: on the main road from Albert to Peronne looking north-west. Description: view of British and German trenches to the east of Mametz with German shellfire. Soldiers in a shell-damaged trench. Shots: 45.1–3. Stills: Q79505, Q79515. Cameraman: McDowell.**

The dope sheet indicates 2 July but again this footage may have been taken on 1 July. Shots 45.1 and 2 were taken from the main road above Minden Post looking towards Mametz and the ridge to the east of the village. The first shot shows the road disappearing down the hill towards the front line. It passes through an embankment which can still be seen. The copse on the extreme left of 45.1 still exists and Fricourt Wood is on the skyline in the distance. The trench in the picture crosses the road through a tunnel and may be Minden Avenue.

*Shot 45.3 may have been taken around the same time. It shows a very battered trench, possibly Minden Avenue. One of the soldiers has 7 Division's pink flannel square on his small pack.* (IWM Q79505)

**Date: 1–4 July 1916. Place: probably the British front line in front of Mametz. Description: men of 2 Royal Warwickshire Regiment moving up to relieve 2 Queen's Regiment. Shot: 33.1. Still: DH82. Cameraman: McDowell.**

The dope sheet allocates this footage to McDowell but gives no location. The battalion shown is 2 Royal Warwickshire Regiment, identified by the 7 Division pink flannel material. The men are laden with all the paraphernalia of front-line infantrymen. Two men wear the white strip of cloth denoting a wire cutter, and the second is carrying a set in his right hand. The battalion was in divisional reserve on 1 July; the *Official History* is at variance with the war diary and states that two companies were sent up during the afternoon to help 1 South Staffordshire Regiment and 21 Manchester Regiment at the eastern end of Mametz village. We know 2 Queen's were in this area at the time so it is quite possible that McDowell was given slightly wrong information when he asked where the troops were going. The war diary records that B and C Companies left the front line at 2.30pm to reinforce 2 Gordons. Alternatively the shot may have been taken in the morning or early afternoon of 4 July when 2 Royal Warwickshire Regiment relieved 2 Queen's in the front line but the weather was very wet that day and there is no sign of rain.[10]

*No screen grab or still exists for this sequence.* Sir Douglas Haig's great push *has this very similar photograph which is from a piece of film no longer in the existing print but extant in the later compilation entitled* The Holmes Lecture Film *(IWM Film and Video Archive 468/3).* (DH82)

**Date: 1 July 1916. Place: the old British front line on the hillside between Mametz and Carnoy. Description: escorts, wounded and prisoners moving back from the front line. Shots: 35.8, 36.1–11, 47.1. Stills: DH95, DH96. Cameraman: McDowell.**

After he had finished filming at Minden Post it seems likely that McDowell followed a marked path over the old British front line on the hillside between Carnoy and Mametz. There he met British soldiers with about eighty prisoners. Here and slightly to the west he took over two minutes of film which forms the whole of caption 36. Another thirty seconds taken in the same place comprises shot 47.1. Shot 35.8 shows wheeled stretchers and seems to match the terrain in this area. The dope sheet attributes caption 36 to Malins 'between La Boisselle and Contalmaison' on 1 July 1916.

*Prisoners being brought in by 10 Worcestershire Regiment at La Boisselle, dated 3 July 1916. The fifth man from the left in the trench has badges similar to those seen in shots 36.1–11 and 47.1. The German army rarely used anything resembling the British battle patch system that came in from 1916 onwards. Two men seem to be wearing the distinctive collar lace of III/109 RIR, although that unit was not holding this sector. The terrain seems to fit the La Boisselle area better than the Montauban ridge and we believe that the caption is correct, but one can easily understand how Malins might have become confused.*
(IWM Q763)

However, the latter village did not fall until 10 July and we suggest that this is an example of Malins' memory failing him. One line of prisoners no doubt looked very much like another. The position is a short walk from Minden Post down into the Carnoy valley and up the far slope; no source other than the dope sheet suggests that Malins was in the area at this time.

The first shot of prisoners is 36.1, which shows a stretcher carried by German medics as well as a number of wounded and tattered prisoners. One man is undoubtedly from 109 RIR and has an unidentified cloth badge on his left upper sleeve. It is possible that these badges were used by 28 Reserve Division perhaps to indicate battalions within a regiment.

The next five shots were all filmed from the same position with a single strand of wire on poles which seems to denote a track. The viewing notes suggest that the 'Lancashire battalion' is probably 21 or 22 Manchester Regiment. 21 Manchester's war diary reads: 'A Coy followed the first battalion over to clean up German front lines and send back prisoners.'[11] The same mysterious badge is evident on men of 109 RIR and what we believe to be 23 IR. In shot 36.3 a group of British soldiers stopped to pose in front of the camera with two prisoners; all seem to be in good spirits and are smiling. Two men from 109 RIR even left the column and circled round to come past the camera twice. Two stretcher-bearers acted as master of ceremonies and played up for the camera, one having a German pipe that he had acquired. It seems to be a slightly hysterical lark between men who were trying to kill each other an hour or two before. McDowell probably moved slightly further down the hill to take shot 36.11, which shows British troops following the track towards the camera.

Shots 36.6–10 were probably shot to the left of the previous ones. They show prisoners carrying stretchers down the hill with two Germans helping a British soldier with a serious head wound which has been dressed. Again the Germans are a mixture of 109 RIR and probably 23 IR. The guard in shot 36.6 is discussed below as he appears in another shot.

Shot 36.11 shows a group of British infantrymen coming down the hillside led by a sergeant, bringing with them two German prisoners. One man at least has a badge either painted on or attached to his helmet, which could be that of the Manchester Regiment, thus making them 21 or 22 Manchester Regiment. They are wearing 1914 pattern equipment which suggests a New Army identity. Caption 47 begins with a shot in the same location on the hillside. The dope sheet gives Malins as the cameraman, the date as 2 or 3 July and the location as La Boisselle, which is all incorrect. Malins did take some footage of prisoners in that area which is not seen in the film and this may be another instance of him getting muddled. The second segment does appear to have been shot on 2 July by Malins and is discussed in Chapter 9.

There are about forty prisoners including some wounded. Men of 109 RIR are again in evidence, many wearing the rectangular cloth badges seen elsewhere. A group of German medical personnel pass the camera, including a medical officer wearing an unusual high-crowned cap of the type sometimes seen worn by Baden

*The area shown in shots 35.8, 36.1–11 and 47.1 in 2007, with Mametz in the left distance as a reference point.*

troops. Another example appears in Q763 (see p. 125). The direction from which the column is coming suggests that the prisoners are from III/109 RIR and many have collar or cuff distinctions of that regiment. The dressing station of III/109 RIR was overrun during the fighting. The battalion medical officer, Dr Karl Bucher, was killed but Assistant Arzt der Reserve Hans Blumers was captured and may be the man seen here.[12]

**Date: 1 July 1916. Place: German trench on the hillside between Carnoy and Mametz. Description: escort and wounded German followed by stretcher-bearers and wounded British soldier. Shot: 35.4. Stills: DH94, Q65411–65412, IWM FLM 1660. Cameraman: McDowell.**

Shot 35.4 shows a British soldier who also appears in shot 36.6. The whole of caption 35 is attributed to Malins in the dope sheet but as this soldier is known to have been on the hillside between Carnoy and Mametz, almost certainly on 1 July 1916, it is

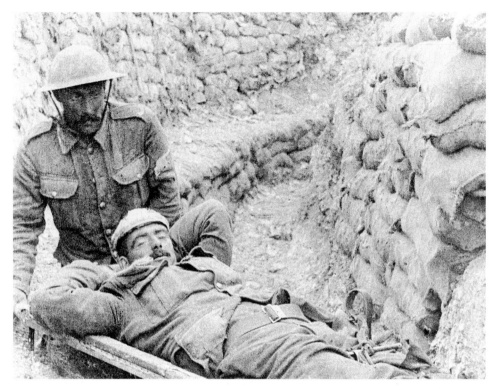

*Two stretcher-bearers bringing the casualty down a trench in the German lines between Carnoy and Montauban.* (IWM Q65412)

unlikely that this footage belongs to Malins. Presumably McDowell had gone further forward and filmed this shot in the German trenches. The British soldier is helping a German from 109 RIR who is wounded in the leg. On the British soldier's helmet cover is an illegible stencilled badge. Behind him are two stretcher-bearers with a British soldier who has a tourniquet on his left leg. He is wearing a helmet liner and seems quite calm despite his wound.

This piece of film seems to be linked to a curious story reported in the Northern Section of *Screen* magazine on 14 October 1916:

A remarkable but pathetic incident occurred on Monday afternoon last at the Droylsden Electric Theatre whilst the official war film *The Battle of the Somme* was being shown. One of the scenes depicted the recovery of wounded in 'No-man's-land' and stretcher-bearers were shown carrying out the wounded when suddenly a woman in the audience leapt to her feet crying 'It's Jim, my husband!' This was Mrs Wilson of 11 Lloyd Street, Droylsden. She had previously received notice that her husband had been killed in action on July 6 and knowing that it was in the advance on the Somme she went to the matinee at the theatre hoping, yet almost afraid, that she might possibly get a glimpse of him but to see him actually carried out on a stretcher made it quite tragic. A good number of the other people in the audience also recognised it as Mr Wilson. Mrs Wilson has been left a widow with nine children.[13]

James Barker Wilson was married to Gertrude Wilson and was 38 years old. *Soldiers died in the Great War* confirms that he had enlisted in Droylsden near Manchester although he came from Nottingham. This would appear to supply a clear identification but the facts do not quite fit. James Wilson served in 10 Lancashire Fusiliers of 17 Division which was part of XV Corps. The film was certainly shot on 1 July 1916 when James Wilson and 10 Lancashire Fusiliers were in the Bois des Tailles. They came into the line near Fricourt on 3 July and James Wilson was killed on 6 July, possibly during a bombing fight in Pearl Alley near Mametz Wood; he is commemorated on the Thiepval Memorial. How therefore does he appear seriously wounded on a stretcher nearly a week before and in a place where his battalion had never been? The conclusion must be that when Gertrude Wilson went to the cinema that day hoping against hope to see her husband on the screen, she saw somebody who closely resembled him. The film was shot 'on the Somme' and the man on the stretcher looked like her Jim, therefore it *was* him. The confirmation from friends in the audience may have been prompted by a desire to help a grieving woman. This story tells us a great deal about the motives, hopes and fears of the audiences of 1916, whose connection with this film was very far from academic. To see one's grandfather on film is a curious feeling, as Anne Dawson discovered; for Gertrude Wilson to see a man she believed to be her husband lying wounded and dying on a stretcher must have been more like seeing a ghost.

**Date: 2 July 1916. Place: north of the D938 by Mansel Copse. Description: 18-pounder guns and limbers of 12 and 25 Batteries, Royal Field Artillery waiting to move up. Shots: 37.1–3. Stills: DH100, Q79503. Cameraman: McDowell.**

Described by the dope sheet as having been shot by McDowell 'on the ridge between Mametz and Carnoy' on 1 July, these three shots were actually taken on 2 July just below Mansel Copse in what had been no-man's-land. The footage shows some of the ground seen in shots 12.3–8 filmed by McDowell before 1 July. A distant view is also found in shots 45.1–2 taken from Minden Post. Shot 37.1 was taken from the bottom of the bank and McDowell then moved up to the top. At the start of shot 37.1 a gun team is seen coming down the road in front of Mansel Copse, the north-east and north-west faces of which are visible. It crosses the main road and turns back to head towards the camera. The first team seems to be drawn by mules and shot 37.2 shows a number of horses in very poor condition. The team passes the body of a Gordon Highlander, killed the previous day. Several other bodies are visible, probably from 9 Devonshire

*Screen grab from shot 37.3 showing a team returning towards the main road.*
(IWM Q79503)

*The same scene in 2007.*

Regiment, which was on the left of the Gordons. Shot 37.1 shows the terrain over which the Gordons and Devons attacked from left to right parallel with the road. The Devons had to get across the shallow valley on the right of the shot and entered the German trenches on the ridge. These can just be made out as a faint white line below the horizon. Both battalions were vulnerable to the machine gun in the shrine, discussed in Chapter 5.

The two batteries are probably 12 and 25 Batteries of 35 Brigade, Royal Artillery, serving with 7 Division. On 2 July the brigade had been ordered to be ready to move at noon and at 2.15pm 25 Battery advanced past Mansel Copse. 12 Battery moved off a few minutes later and at 2.45 both were in the valley at 'F11C', precisely where McDowell was filming. They had to wait while bridges were built to get the guns over the German trenches. We do not know when the bridges were finished but the guns were in action somewhere further north at 7.15pm. The guns are Mk I 18-pounders, the standard British divisional artillery piece of the Great War. All the personnel are wearing service dress caps rather than steel helmets, which were not universal issue at this period.[14]

This footage was the first showing British dead ever to be seen, or indeed to be shown until the end of the next war. The filming of the dead was a subject that provoked strong reactions. The lack of any wounded in the shot suggests they had been cleared before the guns came up. The chaplain to 8 and 9 Devons, Ernest Crosse, tells how at about 3.30pm on 1 July he walked down the road from Mansel Copse; 'the road was strewn with dead', he remarked. 'In every shell hole across the valley and up to the German saps were badly wounded.'[15] Crosse helped to clear these men back to 67 Support Trench which was where the RAP was situated, and from where the bearers from 22 Field Ambulance were picking up the wounded. He was particularly upset that the RAMC took all their stretchers back with the wounded, forcing the regimental medical staff to put men on trench ladders. It will be recalled that the men of 22 Field Ambulance at Minden Post were equally short of stretchers themselves.

Siegfried Sassoon witnessed the attack on Fricourt and passed this way on 2 July with his battalion and saw 'arranged by the roadside, about fifty of the British dead. Many of them were Gordon Highlanders. There were Devons and South Staffordshires among them, but they were beyond regimental rivalry now – their fingers mingled in blood-stained bunches, as though acknowledging the companion-ship of death.'[16] The Gordons collected up their dead on 2 July. They lost 6 officers and 119 other ranks killed and 39 missing. The officers and 93 of the men are buried in Gordon Cemetery on the site of the support trench close to the main road and just visible in shot 12.3. The Devons gathered their dead during 2 and 3 July and carried them up to Mansel Copse. There was a ceremony at 6pm on 4 July attended by about sixty men of the battalion. The original sign, according to Chaplain Ernest Crosse, read 'Cemetery of 163 Devons killed 1 July 1916', which was replaced by the more famous 'The Devonshires held this trench. The Devonshires hold it still.'

**Date: 2 July 1916? Place: valley north of Mansel Copse. Description: line of Highlanders and gunners with an 18-pounder gun. Shot: 59.3. Still: DH154. Cameraman: McDowell?**

This piece of film is not likely to be resolved. It shows Highlanders and Royal Artillery gunners in front of limbered gun teams with an 18-pounder appearing at the end of the shot. Caption 58 is credited to Malins and the first two shots are clearly taken at White City on 1 July, although the dope sheet gives 9 July which is obviously wrong. The Gordons do not seem to have worn kilt aprons on 1 July and the tartan is similar. It is possible that this film was also shot on 2 July at the same time as shots 37.1–3 but we offer this as a possibility rather than a definitive identification.[17]

**Date: 2 July 1916? Place: hillside east of Mametz? Description: 18-pounder battery in action. Distant shot of battery with dead horses in foreground. Shots: 24.1–4. Still: DH61. Cameraman: McDowell.**

The caption reads 'a field battery brought up across the captured German trenches in action within 2 hours of the Germans retiring'. In addition the dope sheet gives the

*The gun pits are well constructed compared to most seen in the film. Some of the gunners have steel helmets which were absent in the previous footage but there were plenty available on the battlefield. (DH61)*

*A screen grab from shot 48.2.* (DH141)

date and the location as 1 July near Mametz. The British do not seem to have got artillery into the German positions on 1 July and the footage was probably taken the next day and may show one of the batteries seen in caption 37. In 7 Division only the batteries of 35 Brigade moved up on 2 July, which suggests that it is one of these. McDowell may have followed them forward after filming them near Mansel Copse. 12 and 25 Batteries were in action just north-west of the Carnoy to Mametz road from the early evening.[18]

**Date: 2–3 July 1916? Place: Danzig Alley area south-west of Mametz. Description: British soldiers, possibly 8 Devonshire Regiment, consolidating the German trenches. Distribution of post. Shots: 48.1–4. Stills: DH138, DH141, Q79517. Cameraman: McDowell?**
There are a number of scenes that we suggest were filmed by McDowell, although there is not always a great deal of evidence. Caption 48 shows the German trenches occupied by British soldiers. The first two shots are difficult to pin down but the distribution of post may have been filmed to the south-west of Mametz near the junction of Orchard Trench and Danzig Alley. The troops may be 8 Devons, who from 2 to 4 July were holding the area around Bunny Alley, Orchard Trench North, the Sunken Road and Orchard Trench, which is as the caption says 'between Fricourt and Mametz'. Their job was 'consolidation, burying the dead and clearing the battlefield', although there is not much work going on.[19] It is possible that these shots and the subsequent footage of the post being distributed were taken at the west end of Danzig or Dantzig Alley, but there is virtually nothing visible for comparison.

**Date: 2–3 July 1916. Place: west of Mametz. Description: dead British and German soldiers. Shots: 50.1–9. Stills: DH141–143, Q65444–65447, Q79519–79521. Cameraman: McDowell.**
Although the dope sheet attributes the first five shots of this caption to McDowell and

*The* Durham County Advertiser *of 22 September 1916 reported 'there is one picture in this film that perhaps brings more tears and "ahs" from the audience than any other. It is of the Manchesters' pet dog and his master lying dead together on the field.'*
(IWM Q79519)

the remaining footage to Malins, we believe that all this footage was shot by McDowell. Caption 50 is not credited to either cameraman but we suggest McDowell filmed the first five shots on the basis that the location is not far from other shots known to have been taken by him.

Shot 50.1 shows a dog and a British soldier lying dead. His small pack has the pink flannel material of 7 Division. The viewing notes suggest a member of 21 or 22 Manchester Regiment, but he was probably one of 20 Manchesters who was killed in that battalion's assault on the western end of Mametz on the afternoon of 1 July. The dog may belong to the battalion commander, Lieutenant Colonel Harold Lewis, although the body may not be that of Lewis himself. Harold Lewis was the son of a captain in the Indian Army and had been commissioned in the 37 Lancers (Baluch Horse). He was home on leave in August 1914 and eventually commanded 20 Manchester Regiment. The battalion had been raised in August 1914 as 5 City Battalion and had joined 22 Brigade, 7 Division in November 1915. 20 Manchesters were tasked with carrying out the final phase of the attack on Fricourt and Mametz by attacking up the Willow Stream valley. Although initial reports were encouraging, the enemy defences had not been entirely suppressed and the units on the flanks of the proposed advance had not yet got on to their objectives. The battalion went over the top from the trenches west of Bois Français at 2.30pm. Harold Lewis was not supposed to accompany his men and is recorded as watching them and remarking 'Isn't it wonderful?' The attack was to comprise A and B Companies of 20 Manchesters with some bombers of 1 Royal Welch Fusiliers, an extraordinarily small number of men for such a task. The attack stalled and according to a family story Colonel Lewis went forward carrying a walking stick, 'unarmed and as though setting off for a country walk', with his dog at his side, in an attempt to get things moving again. Both were killed by machine-gun fire from the direction of Caterpillar Wood. In 1916 Lewis's niece went to see *The Battle of the Somme* and recognised the bodies of the dog and his master.[20]

Shot 50.2 was taken in a trench and shows two or possibly three corpses. It is impossible to say where the shots might have been taken but the trenches south of Mametz are a reasonable guess. There are more shots of German dead, a single body and another with four men shown. All the men lie among the heavily battered German trenches and have no weapons or equipment discernible.

Shot 50.5 shows a dead British soldier crouched down on his haunches in front of a sandbagged wall in a trench. Q65445 has the caption 'a British soldier killed in a trench between Montauban and Carnoy', which would fit with the dope sheet. This has the heading 'Scenes on the battlefield. A battalion of the Middlesex Regiment burying German dead', with the location 'Montauban and Carnoy'. This may suggest that the shot was taken by Malins, who is credited with these scenes. However, there is evidence that Malins did not film in this area until 5 July. It is almost certain that the man died on 1 July 1916 and a pathologist's opinion is that from the condition of

*Grab from shot 50.2 showing two or possibly three corpses including a British soldier in the foreground.* (IWM Q65444)

*Unknown British soldier near Mametz.* (IWM Q65445)

the body he was filmed within thirty-six hours of death. Thus the footage must have been shot by McDowell. It is impossible to say who this soldier might be. Tantalisingly he has something written on his helmet cover. Three letters are visible, of which the final two may be 'ER'. The writing of personal names on helmet covers was rare in the British Army of the Great War and the word could be a designation such as 'bomber'. The man's left hand is discoloured from livor mortis (the pooling of the blood in the lower extremities after death). He may be held in position by rigor mortis and there are instances of bodies remaining in a similar crouching posture for years.

The next forty-five seconds of footage shows German dead being buried. The burial party was almost certainly from 12 Middlesex, 18 Division. They were in reserve on 1 July but moved up in the afternoon to Bund, Emden and Triangle trenches and the next day to White Trench, Beetle Alley and Maple Trench. During 2 July 'the dead were collected and buried within our area'. The Germans are probably from III/109 RIR and were killed in the morning or early afternoon of 1 July. Using forensic techniques and temperature records from Fourth Army headquarters it is possible to get an estimate of the time at which the bodies were filmed. Some men

*Screen grab of German dead being buried. Rigor mortis is still present in the corpse in the foreground.* (DH143)

still have stiff limbs while one man is limp. The two main factors affecting decomposition are temperature and insects, although there is no evidence of the latter. The progress of decay is measured in Accumulated Degree Days using the temperature data. Thus 100 ADD could mean 5 days at 20 degrees C or 20 days at 5 degrees C. The stage of decomposition will be the same at 100 ADD, no matter how many days it took to reach that figure. The ADD calculation gives a Total Body Score which is a set of decay characteristics. Matching these against the condition of the corpse provides an accurate estimation of the time of death under the prevailing temperature conditions. The TBS of the corpses in the footage is three or four, which tells us they were filmed some twenty-four to thirty-six hours after death and therefore most likely on 2 July. On this day Malins was either at Acheux or outside La Boisselle so he cannot have taken this footage.[21]

**Date: 2 July 1916? Place: eastern outskirts of Mametz. Description: right pan across men resting in a trench. A wrecked trench mortar emplacement. Shots: 39.1–2. Stills: DH112, DH113, Q65415–65416. Cameraman: McDowell.** The dope sheet states that this footage was filmed by McDowell on 2 July near Mametz. The viewing notes identify the battalion as 22 Manchesters. Their war diary records them as being in Danzig Alley by the end of 1 July. The next day they also

*The men seem to be quite relaxed although many are carrying weapons or have them close at hand. One man is wearing a pickelhaube and the pink flannel sign of 7 Division is visible on two small packs.* (IWM Q65415–65416)

*The probable location of shot 39.1 at the eastern end of Mametz. Further west Danzig Alley drops away down the slope. Men of both Manchester battalions were in this area which suggests that we are as near as the available evidence allows.*

took over Bright Alley which runs north out of the village and has a junction with Danzig Alley. 21 Manchesters had their battalion headquarters in Mametz and the commanding officer Lieutenant Colonel W.W. Norman was in command of the garrison. Elements were also in Danzig Alley so the troops seen could be from either battalion. Buildings are visible on the pan which suggests the east end of the village before Danzig Alley follows the Montauban road up the ridge. Getting accurate comparison shots in Fricourt and Mametz proved to be extremely difficult. As both villages were reduced to rubble and ground levels have changed considerably during rebuilding, the only clues are skylines and more distant terrain features which are frequently obscured by buildings and trees.[22]

Shot 39.2 has no features that might provide a location and we accept the dope sheet location of 'near Mametz'. It shows a heavy trench mortar in an emplacement with the overhead cover of corrugated iron sheets displaced by shell damage.

There is no footage after 3 July 1916 that we can clearly attribute to McDowell, although equally no evidence that he returned to London before 10 July. Whether he suffered camera problems or was unable to get more film we do not know.

## CHAPTER NINE

# MALINS AFTER 1 JULY 1916

**Date: 2 July 1916. Place: railway sidings south of Acheux. Description: German prisoners in cage; prisoners being marched to railway wagons and embarking. Shots: 47.2–3, 62.1–3. Stills: DH158. Q732. Cameraman: Malins.**
The dope sheet states that these shots were taken on 2 or 3 July 1916 by Malins at Albert. Shots 47.2–3 are described by the caption as 'Prisoners in compound awaiting transportation', while caption 62, following from caption 61, is entitled 'Whilst "others" less fortunate depart under escort for England'. There is no doubt that Malins was the cameraman and we suggest 2 July as being the more likely date but the location is certainly not Albert, which did not have a functioning railway station in 1916 and was well within artillery range of the front line. Q732, captioned 'Battle of Albert. German prisoners at Acheux, July 1916' is the first clue to the correct location because it was clearly taken at the same time as shots 47.2–3. Malins tells how he stayed in the White City area until sometime on 2 July when he heard that things were going better elsewhere and decided to leave. 'I got safely back through the trenches to . . . , where Brigade HQ told me of an urgent message from GHQ. I was told to report as soon as possible. On my way back I called on General . . . , who was delighted to hear I had successfully filmed the attack, the record of which would show the world how gloriously our men had fought.' The probable course of events was that Malins went back to 86 Brigade HQ in Mailly-Maillet where he received a message to report to Advanced GHQ. It is likely that he called on General de Lisle, whose main divisional headquarters was in Acheux, and he probably filmed this footage while passing through the town. He presumably reported to Faunthorpe at Advanced GHQ at Chateau Val Vion in Beauquesne and was told to go to La Boisselle. He may have picked up his Aeroscope camera from here and possibly handed over his exposed film before motoring back to Albert.[1]

The prisoner-of-war compound seen in shot 47.2–3 was in the field south of the metre-gauge railway line that used to run round Acheux. Railway wagons can be seen in the background of both shots and Acheux church and a factory chimney are also visible. These features can be seen on a 1916 map and enabled us to fix the location precisely. Acheux was a major railhead for the northern sector of the Somme front. The station gave access to extensive standard- and metre-gauge railway systems, some of which had been inherited from the French and much constructed by the British Army.

The men in shot 47.2 are mainly dressed in M1910 tunics or the transitional pattern with plain cuffs. As at Minden Post the sun is a problem and some men have

*German prisoners lying in the sun waiting for transport to take them to the rear. The trees in the background run along the railway embankment.* (IWM Q732)

*The site of the prisoner-of-war compound in 2007. The railway line is now a footpath.*

improvised caps from paper. A few have used handkerchiefs for the same purpose. Shot 47.3 shows the prisoners getting ready to move out of the cage to the railway wagons.

We believe that these men are from 99 RIR. This regiment was formed of men from Alsace and the Rhineland. On mobilisation it was allocated to 26 Reserve Division from Württemberg and was not immediately welcomed, the Alsatians in particular being viewed with suspicion. In the area served by the Acheux railhead the only large capture of prisoners was by 36 (Ulster) Division between Thiepval and St Pierre Divion. 109 Brigade managed to overrun the German front line fairly easily and many men from 9 and 10 Companies of III/99 RIR were captured before they could offer much resistance. Cyril Falls gives the total of prisoners as 543, which is not far from the 400 or so in shots 62.1–2.[2] The history of 99 RIR's service on the Somme records that 11 officers and 624 NCOs and men were missing or captured between 24 June and 31 July. During that period 59 officers and 2,482 other ranks were removed from the strength by all causes. This amounts to a loss of over 75 per cent of the effective strength and is a reminder that it was not only British battalions that were suffering.[3]

Caption 62 comprises three shots showing the prisoners on their way to the railway wagons and being loaded. There is a large crowd of onlookers including some wearing 29 Division patches. There is a contrast in the attitudes of both prisoners and captors compared to those seen in the shots taken by McDowell. The men of 99 RIR are a formed body of men. There is no friendly interaction between them and the British spectators who are not front-line soldiers; they are curious about the prisoners, as can be seen by the men hurrying across the railway lines to look at the column in shot 62.2. There is no overt hostility but none of the overexcited horseplay that McDowell filmed. The escort are cavalrymen from VIII Corps Cavalry Regiment. This was formed by 1/1 Lancashire Hussars Yeomanry on 11 May 1916 and one man can be seen wearing a cap badge of the right shape for that regiment. Unfortunately the regimental war diary for July 1916 is missing but on 30 June a troop under Captain Aspinall proceeded from Orville to Acheux to act as escorts for prisoners.[4] Shot 62.3 shows a group of about thirty men getting into a goods wagon on the sidings and is the final shot in the film with the exception of a later map of the Allied advance up to 11 April 1917. This map has been omitted from the DVD of the film issued by the Imperial War Museum.

## Malins at La Boisselle

Up to this point it is not difficult to separate the footage shot by Malins and McDowell. If a shot can be fixed by location and date it can be safely ascribed to one or other cameraman. The dope sheet gives the impression that after 2 July 1916 both men then worked in the same area and that both took footage around Mametz and Fricourt. We have some doubts that this is a true record of events. In his book Malins indicates that

*Three grabs showing shots 62.1–3.* (DH158)

he did not go further south than the La Boisselle area at any point. This book was written in 1917 and therefore predates the dope sheet, which appears to have been put together between 1918 and 1920 and was certainly in existence in 1922. Caption 62 has been added to the end of the dope sheet in a different typeface and seems to be an alteration to reflect the later running order as it exists in the print that survives today rather than the original release print. We cannot be sure how the dope sheet was compiled. We do not know if it was produced at a showing of the film or from other documentation. Usually a list of shots went in the can with the exposed film, so it could have been based upon such notes. It is also uncertain who was responsible for its compilation, although there is one faint clue. Malins is referred to throughout as 'Captain Malins', a rank by which he was known in the post-war period. This suggests that whoever assembled the dope sheet either knew him as Captain Malins or Malins himself made the attributions. It seems strange that Malins would fail to recount his exploits in the Mametz and Montauban areas but he never mentions getting further south than Bécourt Wood before heading back to London. The account in *How I filmed the war* ends rather abruptly after he recounts the story of his missing orderly and it is possible that he skipped the trip south, perhaps either because it lacked excitement or he needed to cut his narrative. However, the dope sheet has a cluster of sequences attributed to Malins which suggests that he made a trip to Carnoy and Montauban on 5 July and we know he was in Bécordel on 6 July and Fricourt on 8 July. These shots do not show any corpses, unlike the footage shot by McDowell, which may indicate that the visible parts of the battlefield had been cleared by the time Malins got there. When one considers the amount of footage that he took from 1914 to 1918 it is plausible that he could not remember in detail and that the misattributions are accidental rather than deliberate. The film is one of three that he shot on the Somme between July and October 1916.

Malins suggests that he got to the La Boisselle area sometime on 2 July but we believe that all the surviving footage dates from 3 July. He describes stopping the car at the top of Bécourt Wood. Malins took one camera, probably the Moy and Bastie, and gave the Aeroscope to one helper and the tripod to the other. Although he does not mention him, Malins was accompanied by Ernest Brooks, who took a number of stills. Malins set off immediately to begin filming but got badly lost, having no map of the area. Under heavy shelling he was desperate to get some footage but was seen and fired on by the Germans. Eventually he found some German prisoners to film and although there is no surviving footage there are some stills showing prisoners from La Boisselle taken by Ernest Brooks. All are dated 3 July 1916. Malins describes looking for one of his assistants as it came on to rain heavily. The weather broke on the evening of 3 July, which also strengthens the case for dating the footage to that day.

**Date: 3 July 1916? Place: Usna Hill to the east of the Albert to Bapaume road. Description: barrage in progress on the horizon followed by scenes of**

**wounded returning from the front line. Shots: 38.1–4, 34.4. Stills: DH86, DH114, Q770, Q774. Cameraman: Malins.**

The four shots in this caption were all taken within a fairly small area and probably at the same time. Shots 38.3–4 can be linked to photographs taken by Ernest Brooks. The dope sheet wrongly claims that Malins filmed this footage near Poziéres on 9 July. A grab of shot 38.1 in *How I filmed the war* is captioned 'The Germans made a big counter-attack at La Boisselle and Ovillers. July 3 and 4, 1916.' The only German counter-attack over this period was carried out by 190 IR of 185 Infantry Division, which is mentioned in both British and German sources. By 3 July the garrison of La Boisselle, 110 RIR, was desperately hanging on to the northern end of the village. An attack was launched to relieve them and eject the British from La Boisselle. 190 IR came under heavy British barrage fire which is probably what we see in these two shots. One column was forced to turn back towards Poziéres but contrary to what the caption tells us elements of two other columns made it into La Boisselle and succeeded in driving the British back slightly.[5] Shots 38.1–2 were taken from the same position on the forward slope of Usna Hill.

Shots 38.2–3 show a group of stretcher-bearers carrying a casualty away from La Boisselle. The bombardment carries on in the background, suggesting that the two

*Possibly the same bombardment as seen in shot 38.1.* (IWM Q774)

*La Boisselle, which is on the left, was the objective of 190 IR. The shells were falling on the ridge line from the middle to the left of this photograph.*

*A shot dated 3 July 1916 and taken by Ernest Brooks. The figure on the left of the shot is Malins himself filming stretcher-bearers, who may be those seen in shots 37.2–3.*

(IWM Q770)

scenes have been shot with little time in between. Malins has moved west to the edge of the main Albert to Bapaume road.

Shot 34.4 was probably taken at around the same time and shows two teams of stretcher-bearers, one with a wheeled stretcher carrier. This shot may have been taken on the Albert to Bapaume road near the site of Bapaume Post cemetery.

**Date: 3–5 July 1916? Place: Lochnagar Crater, La Boisselle. Description: scene from western edge of mine crater. Shots: 29.5–6, 51.3–4. Stills: DH145, Q79522, IWM FLM 1659. Cameraman: Malins.**

This footage appears in the video release of the film as part of caption 29 following the footage of the Hawthorn Ridge mine exploding. It has been omitted from the DVD version. The crater seen here was created by the Lochnagar mine, which was detonated under the Schwaben Redoubt or Schwaben Höhe, east of La Boisselle, at 7.28am on 1 July 1916. The mine comprised two charges of 36,000 and 24,000 pounds of ammonal in two separate chambers, and according to a German account the shower of stones continued for nearly a minute after the explosion. Although several dugouts collapsed the defenders were not put out of action to any great extent and managed to inflict heavy casualties among the attacking troops of 34 Division.[6]

The footage appears again, with rather more justification, as shots 51.3–4, as part of the caption entitled 'The devastating effect of British shell fire. Smashed trenches and dugouts. A mine crater 40 feet deep.' The dope sheet gives the date as 5 July 1916 and the location as 'near La Boisselle and Montauban', with Malins as the cameraman. It was probably filmed with the other shots taken in the same area on 3 July. However, even by 5 July the area was still not exactly safe for sight-seeing so it is conceivable that he filmed it some days later, perhaps between 7 and 9 July, the latter probably being his last day of filming. The camera position is on the western edge of the crater looking towards the far side of Sausage Valley, and the shots show the vast scale of this feature. A party of troops can be seen in the distance on the other side of the valley. The kilted soldier and the man wearing a trench coat, presumably an officer, appear in shots 51.1–2 and 49.1 which may indicate that all this footage was shot by Malins, despite the dope sheet attributing caption 49 to McDowell. However, the identity of these two men remains a mystery: Malins does not mention being accompanied by anyone except a couple of anonymous orderlies, one of whom may have been David Laing. It is not clear if he had a conducting officer with him.

**Date: 3–5 July 1916? Place: west side of Sausage Valley, La Boisselle. Description: two anonymous figures inspecting battered German trenches. Shots: 51.1–2. Cameraman: Malins.**

These two shots show the two figures seen in 51.3–4 walking through a shell crater about 15 feet deep. The second shot shows the two men wandering among some extremely badly damaged trenches. There are very few clues as to location but the valley in the distance seems to fit the west side of Sausage Valley. Trees can be seen

*A grab from the film showing the face of the crater with two figures on the rim and another coming up from the bottom.* (IWM FLM 1659)

*The approximate site of the camera position in 2007, with the view somewhat obscured by foliage.*

on the horizon which may be those lining the Contalmaison to Fricourt road. The road is shown on 1916 maps as being partly tree lined although it is not known for certain if these trees would have been visible from where we suspect the photograph was taken.

**Date: 3–5 July 1916? Place: Sausage Valley area, La Boisselle? Description: dead German soldiers in a shell crater. Shot: 49.1. Stills: Q65441–65442, Q79518. Cameraman: Malins.**

The dope sheet states that caption 49 was shot by McDowell between 1 and 3 July between Montauban and Carnoy but we suggest that it was in fact taken by Malins at about the same time as the previous shots around Lochnagar crater. The lower halves of the Highlander and trench-coated man described above can be seen. This shot shows a shell crater full of German corpses.

*Some of these bodies have been grabbed by their hands and feet and flung into the crater. German bodies excavated by No-Man's-Land in a trench at the Hohenzollern Redoubt were found in a similar attitude, having been thrown in with an equal lack of ceremony.*
(IWM Q65442)

## Malins in Carnoy and Montauban

Having found his missing assistant, it is probable that Malins made his way south-west towards the Carnoy area, probably on 5 July. The alternative is that he checked with GHQ, as he says in his book, and then returned home and that the footage shot in Carnoy and Montauban was actually taken by McDowell. This seems to us to be the less likely course of events and there is little or no footage attributable to McDowell after 3 July. We do not know exactly when McDowell went back to Britain but it may have been earlier than the accepted date of 10 July. Certainly Malins was back by the Albert to Bapaume road on 8 July to film 13 Royal Fusiliers. There are a considerable number of sequences in the later part of the film for which there is little evidence to attribute credit to either cameraman, and this does make a reliable chronology difficult to achieve; some of our deductions are therefore somewhat tentative!

**Date: 5 July 1916? Place: Carnoy? Description: two Lanz trench mortars being carried in. Shots: 55.1–3. Still: DH149. Cameraman: Malins.**
The dope sheet gives the location as Carnoy and the terrain resembles the bottom end

*Two Lanz-type light trench mortars being carried down a road by gunners.* (DH149)

of the village. There is no real reason to doubt the dope sheet. The Lanz mortar was an effective weapon despite its rather antiquated appearance. It fired a 4kg shell, a box of which is being examined in the background of the shot.

**Date: 5 July 1916? Place: Carnoy? Description: two 77mm field guns and a trench gun being towed past the camera. Shots: 55.4–5. Still: DH150. Cameraman: Geoffrey Malins.**

The main difficulty presented by this footage is the location, although we can at least be sure it is not 'near La Boisselle' as the caption states. It is possible that it is the main road from Montauban to Carnoy and the guns have been taken up the Mametz to Montauban road before turning right down to Carnoy. This would fit the location in the dope sheet but there is no evidence that this road was tree-lined, one would expect to see more damage in an area that had been heavily fought over, and the landscape does not fit.

The two 77mm field guns probably belonged to 3/57 Field Artillery Regiment of 12 Division. On 1 July the only remaining serviceable gun was pulled from its shelter and was fired on the advancing British at a range of 200 metres before the gunners

*One of the guns captured by 7 Division. The officer by the roadside wearing a British warm may be Ernest Brooks, who appears in Q1456 in a similar stance.* (DH150)

abandoned the position. They returned in the evening but found the British in possession of the battery. The war diary of 2 Queen's records that two 77mm guns were found
on 3 July, one of which they were unable to move because of a damaged wheel. One
gun in shot 55.4 has a locked wheel. 7 Division allocated three teams for the recovery
of captured artillery.[7]

**Date: 5 July 1916? Place: Carnoy? Description: Essex Regiment washing at a
pool. Shot: 58.1. Stills: DH153, DH251. Cameraman: Geoffrey Malins?**
The viewing notes not unreasonably associate this shot with 1 Essex of 29 Division,
and the Seaforth Highlanders who appear in the next three shots are undoubtedly from
that formation. We suggest that the first part of the caption may be correct and that
these men are from 10 Essex of 18 Division. *Sir Douglas Haig's great push* has a photograph of this pond from the opposite direction which shows it to be in a badly ruined
village. This does not match anywhere in the 29 Division area and no 29 Division
patches can be seen. The pond may have been in Carnoy but it has proved impossible
to find. 10 Essex Regiment was in the Pommiers area until relieved on 7 July when it
moved back to Bronfay Farm. One interesting point is that a number of men say 'Hello

*Note the trees on the horizon. There are several ruined houses off camera to the right.*
(DH153)

Mum' or 'Hello Mum, it's me' when looking at the camera, demonstrating that they expected to be recognised when the film was shown.

**Date: 5 July 1916? Place: Mametz. Description: various views of the village. Shots: 52.2, 53.1–3. Stills: DH144, DH146, DH147, Q772–773, Q1063. Cameraman: Malins.**
The footage of Mametz is particularly difficult to match to the ground. Shot 52.2 is a circular pan around the village, despite the caption claiming it is Fricourt.

*The building in the centre of the photograph appears at the beginning of shot 52.2.*
(IWM Q773)

*The approximate position in 2007 with the same S-bend in the road.*

Shot 53.1 shows the top end of Mametz from a distance before 53.2 switches to another pan taken further towards the western end of the village. The remains of the church can be seen in the distance. Shot 53.3 is a tighter pan of some shattered houses.

**Date: 5 July 1916? Place: not located. Description: shell-damaged German trench. Shot: 52.3. Still: DH142. Cameraman: Malins.**
This is one of a number of shots that have proved impossible to locate. It shows a German trench with wickerwork revetment. One of the sign-boards appears to read

*A still of the ruined buildings that appear in shot 52.3. (IWM Q772)*

*Another damaged house in Mametz in July 1916. (IWM Q1063)*

'Jurgen . . .' or 'Jungen . . .' but we cannot trace a trench with any similar name from German sources. It is possible that this shot was filmed with 53.4–5 at Fricourt but there is no firm evidence.

**Date: 5 July 1916? Place: Fricourt. Description: two shots of the village taken facing south from the top of the bank by the crossroads at the south entrance to the village. Shots 53.4–5. Stills: DH148, DH166. Cameraman: Malins.**

*There is nothing to link these two shots other than that they were filmed from the top of a bank and show rising ground in the distance. Malins has climbed up the bank above the road leading out of the west side of the village just below the square. The wrecked emplacement seen in the second shot would be well sited to oppose any advance made across the valley to the south. (DH166)*

*The view from the top of the bank in Fricourt back towards the British lines.*

**Date: 5–6 July 1916? Place: the ridge between Montauban and Carnoy. Description: two officers with soldiers clearing an enemy trench for the camera. Shots: 46.1–2. Stills: DH137, Q79516, IWM FLM 1656. Cameraman: Malins.**

We accept the dope sheet attribution to Malins and the approximate location. The date of 1–3 July is probably too early. The trees in the background match those that stood beside the Albert to Bapaume road in 1916, indicating that the location is in the German lines on the ridge north-west of Carnoy. The first shot shows two officers and four men negotiating very badly shattered barbed wire. The second shows the same officers and eight men walking down a trench. The casual attitude of the men in the background confirms that the two scenes were set up for the camera but these troops were certainly front-line infantry. The helmets resemble those seen in shots 6.1–3 in Bray on 30 June with a symbol on the front and the unusual form of draw cord on the helmet cover. This suggests that the troops are from 18 Division, while the collar dog

*A grab from shot 46.2 showing the advance down the trench.*

*The approximate position of this episode in 2008 with Maricourt in the distance on the left.*

on the second officer in shot 46.2 seems to be that of the Bedfordshire Regiment. Two companies of 7 Bedfords were in the German trenches on 3 July while the remainder were in Carnoy and Caftet Wood. On 6 July the entire battalion moved forward to Pommiers and Caterpillar Trench, which would provide another date for the filming. Although it is not completely conclusive, the time and place do fit.[8]

**Date: 6 July 1916. Place: Bécordel. Description: 8-inch howitzer being towed into the village and moved into position. Shots: 60.1–5. Stills: DH160–161, Q794, Q795, Q827. Cameraman: Malins.**
The dope sheet states that this footage was shot by Malins on 5 July 1916 at Bécordel and that the guns shown belong to 56 Siege Battery. The war diary of 56 Siege Battery, however, indicates that nos 1 and 2 guns arrived at Bécordel at 2.30pm on 6 July from their previous positions at Courcelle-au-Bois. It is these pieces we see in the footage as the other two howitzers did not reach there until 10.30pm that evening.[9]

*No. 1 howitzer of 56 Siege Battery in Bécordel on the afternoon of 6 July.* (DH161)

*The same scene in 2007. The curve in the road on the horizon corresponds to the road layout in the film.*

*The first two guns arrived at 2.30pm but it took four hours to get them into the emplacements constructed for them earlier in the day, perhaps not surprisingly considering the difficulty of hauling a 13-ton weight with drag ropes. When both were in position a total of twenty-three rounds were fired on Mash Valley for registration.* (IWM Q794–795)

**Date: 8 July 1916. Place: west of the Albert to Bapaume Road. Description: men of 13 Royal Fusiliers resting after an attack on the north end of La Boisselle. Shots: 56.3, 57.1–5. Stills: DH151–153, Q775–777, Q781, Q797–798, IWM FLM 1648. Cameraman: Malins.**

Shots 57.1–2 show men of an unidentified battalion bivouacked in a valley just south of Ville-sur-Ancre. It is possible but not certain that shot 56.3 of men sleeping in the open with piled arms may be associated. However, shots 57.3–5 are known to be 13 Royal Fusiliers beside the Albert to Bapaume road. The battalion had taken part in an attack on La Boisselle and spent the next two days in the Tara-Usna line near the main road. Judging by the condition of the men, Malins almost certainly filmed them on the morning of 8 July. Corroboration of this comes from Guy Chapman's *Passionate prodigality*. Chapman had been left behind when the battalion went up the line but rejoined

*A still taken at the same time as the ciné footage which confirms Chapman's description: 'Pickelhaubes, German helmets, Teutonic forage caps, leaf-shaped bayonets, automatics, were produced from haversacks. The faces which ten minutes earlier had seemed those of dying men were now alight with excited amusement. "Come on, come an' have your picture took" echoed from man to man: and amid much cheering, the official press was obliged with a sitting.' The souvenirs include a helmet cover of 190 IR, which had survived the barrage shown in caption 37. (IWM Q777)*

*The same spot in 2007. The new buildings make an exact comparison difficult.*

them on that morning. He was talking to one of his friends 'when there was a sudden stir. A few men rose, others woke and joined them, collecting in a mob around a khaki figure with a camera.'[10]

**Date: 8 July 1916. Place: Fricourt. Description: road repairs being made by 12 Duke of Cornwall's Light Infantry. Shot: 52.1. Still: DH148. Cameraman: Malins.**

The damage to Fricourt makes a certain comparison almost impossible but we believe this shot was taken in what remained of the main square looking north. The caption notes the presence of a labour battalion of the Duke of Cornwall's Light Infantry, which offers an important clue; the dope sheet dates the shot to 5 July but the war diary of 12 (Labour) Battalion DCLI records that the battalion was then working on the roads around Grovetown. At 7.30am on the morning of 8 July the commanding officer received a telegram ordering him to send two officers and 150 men to Fricourt. Problems with transport meant that only two lorries with about forty men reached the village at about 1pm. The remainder did not arrive until 5pm.[11]

*The remains of the church can be seen on the right in this grab from* Sir Douglas Haig's
great push. *The men working on the road may be the first party of 12 DCLI to arrive.*
(DH148)

*The view from the south end of the square in Fricourt. Shots 53.4–5 were taken from the
bank on the left and 52.1 was probably shot from the top end of the square looking north.*

CHAPTER TEN

# THE FAKE FOOTAGE

Date: 12–19 July 1916? Place: Third Army Mortar School, Ligny-St-Flochel, near St Pol. Description: two sequences of troops going over the top and shots of shells dropping outside barbed wire. Shots: 'over the top': 31.1–2; shelling sequences: 17.3–6, 27.1 and 29.4. Stills: 'over the top' scenes: DH78–79, DH82, Q65405–65409, Q70164–70169, Q70693, Q70693A, Q70694–70699, Q79500, IWM FLM 1654; shelling scenes: DH69, Q784–785, Q787–788, Q79487. Cameraman: Malins?

One of the most controversial elements of the film is the question of how much is faked. The suspect material includes two scenes of British soldiers going over the top and advancing into the smoke, several men falling as they move forward. This footage is frequently interpreted as showing the 'reality' of the Great War but doubts have been expressed about its authenticity since at least 1922.

It can be argued that one of the reasons for the success of the film was its genuine appearance. Unlike the newsreel material of 1914 and 1915 it was not contrived and showed real soldiers risking their lives. From remarks in contemporary papers it is certain that the audience believed they were watching men die and regarded the film as entirely genuine. The *Durham Advertiser* recounted 'then comes the order for the attack and at a given signal the men, bayonets fixed, leap over the parapets and advance into the heavy fire, two gallant Tommies falling, as it were, at one's feet'.[1] Is there any justification for passing off such faked material as genuine or were the cameramen cynically manipulating the emotions of the audience? As we have seen, filming combat was dangerous and difficult, and Nicholas Hiley makes the seemingly contradictory point that the fakes 'in fact increased the realism of the photographic coverage of the war'.[2]

Although faking was frowned upon by many cameramen it was not clear how it should be defined. Malins said, 'I have tried to make my pictures actual and reliable, above all I have striven to catch the actual atmosphere of the battlefield'.[3] Bertram Brooks Carrington, who was interviewed in 1972 by Kevin Brownlow, denied that he faked shots: 'No, I never did that. It was easy enough to do if you wanted to because there was a trench mortar battery school at St Pol and it would have been easy to reconstruct anything there . . . You just had to get your story. Sometimes exaggerate the story a little bit. No faking. Not in the true sense of the word.'[4]

*The training area at Ligny-St-Flochel with the trees along the Ternais to Averdoingt road in the distance.* (IWM Q787)

*The same view in 2007.*

Quite what the true sense of the word was he does not reveal. When asked about faking he stated: 'I don't think anybody else did. Malins was the only bloke who did that. Apart from early days, the two that were there most of the time McDowell and Raymond wouldn't have attempted anything like that.' Again there is a qualification in his statement as he suggests that scenes were faked 'in the early days', by which he presumably means 1914 and 1915. Hilton de Witt Girdwood appears to have faked combat footage in his film *With the Empire's fighters*, which was shot in 1915; the Australian photographer Frank Hurley created elaborate montages from separate photographs and argued that it was a legitimate practice; and Ivor Castle of the *Daily Mirror* manipulated two sequences of still photographs. One included a shell burst from a picture taken at Ligny-St-Flochel. Ernest Brooks was particularly upset about these faked photographs, which were 'a thing we have strict instructions not to do — we have never done it. We have always taken our chance up amongst the fighting.'[5] On the other hand at least one cameraman, Oscar Bovill, is known to have been dismissed for falsification in 1917.

The story of the 'over the top' sequences and footage purporting to show the bombardment of the German lines at Beaumont Hamel is a complex one. It begins with a statement by Brooks Carrington who remembered:

> Early in '17 we were in a place called Rollencourt, close to St Pol. At St Pol there was a trench mortar battery school and I went in there one day – I was on my way to Arras, got time to spare, sat down and had a cup of coffee, a chap passing by, a serviceman, saw my camera and tripod. He strolled over and said 'Excuse me', he said, 'do you know a Lieut. Malins?' I said 'yes'. He said 'I wonder how his pictures came out'. He said 'he did a lot here at the battery school. I was one of the blokes that fell down dead in the trench.'[6]

The château at Rollencourt was used as a base by press correspondents. The 'trench mortar battery school' was Third Army Trench Mortar School based at Ligny-St-Flochel about 6.5 km east of St Pol. The school has no war diary but was used for the demonstration of weaponry to important personalities including George V. Brooks Carrington described the school as a set of trenches and wire 'laid out in a full-scale model (mock-up) of the real thing. So blokes could practise under conditions that would ensue afterwards.' There is one piece of evidence to back up Brooks Carrington's statement that Malins was at Ligny-St-Flochel at about the time of the 'over the top' sequences.[7]

It is not known if both cameramen were involved in the 'reconstructions' or when the footage was taken. The two men returned to England about 10 July; McDowell was certainly interviewed in his London office that day. They could have stopped at Ligny-St-Flochel on their way to England to re-shoot scenes that they had doubts about. The film must have been developed immediately as it was screened in negative on 12 July, which would hardly have allowed enough time to set up a filming session in France. It seems more likely that one or both men returned to France in the week

*A photograph of Malins at Ligny-St-Flochel. The original caption reads: 'In a shell hole in "no-man's-land" filming our heavy bombardment of the German lines. I got into this position during the night previous. It was here that I earned the soubriquet "Malins of no man's land".' However, this shot cannot be genuine as the tree stump to Malins' left also appears in shot 27.1 from the opposite direction. In later sequences the tree stump is augmented with more barbed wire and appears partly in 29.1 as well, both shots being filmed at Ligny-St-Flochel. Shot 27.1 is captioned as showing shells landing on the German positions. If this is true then Malins would have been in no-man's-land but filming back towards the British lines watching German shells dropping on the British trenches. The conclusion is that Malins is shown on the Ligny-St-Flochel training area either before the Somme filming or at an early stage in a visit to get the 'over the top' scenes before the immediate vicinity had been dressed with more wire.*[8]

after 12 July, having seen the unedited film and knowing which material they had to re-shoot. This was ready by 19 July when the film is known to have been at the editing stage. Malins filmed men going over the top at White City and some of this footage survives in shots 31.3–4 but it may be that the remainder was either unspectacular or too bloody to show. While prepared to show some casualties, simulated or real, the authorities could hardly sanction a film showing two battalions of infantry being cut to pieces. This could be the reason for a more acceptable but still controversial reconstruction of men going over the top. There may also not have been enough genuine footage of shelling. Real shell fire was impossible to orchestrate properly and filming it under controlled conditions would produce a more dramatic effect.

We suggest that the 'over the top' and 'shelling' scenes were shot in the days between 12 and 19 July. The filming required considerable assistance from the army as it involved the participation of several mortars and their crews as well as the provision of smoke, mortar ammunition and about twenty men to masquerade as infantry. Labour would also have been required to add to the existing barbed wire defences.

There are two 'over the top' sequences in the film (shots 31.1–31.2). The first was filmed from the left rear and shows a group of about twenty soldiers equipped with rifles and gas helmets being led over the parapet of a shallow, unrevetted trench by an officer armed with what appears to be a riding crop. One man partly visible on the left of the shot falls back into the trench and his arms and left leg can be seen to move; another man further to the right exposes his head over the parapet for a second, turns his head to the left and then slides back down the side of the trench. Presumably one of these men later spoke to Brooks Carrington. Once out of the trench the men disappear down a slope into smoke which is drifting from right to left. At a showing of the film in 1922 a panel of War Office experts declared this footage to be fake.

The second shot is taken from directly behind and shows about sixteen men led by an officer stepping over a low wire apron and disappearing into smoke which is drifting from left to right. Two men fall among the wire, the left one seemingly crossing his legs after a few seconds, the other still moving slightly. The last man visible continues after his comrades and begins to fall as the shot ends. On the right of the shot can be seen a bayonet belonging to another soldier who would have been standing in the middle of the small-arms fire that has already incapacitated two of his comrades and which would put the cameraman himself at considerable risk. Again the troops, who may be the same men as in the previous shot, have minimal equipment. The smoke hides the surroundings but comparison with the shelling footage reveals that this shot was taken in the same place as shots 27.1 and 29.4. The same barbed wire appears on all three shots and the tree stump which betrayed Malins is also seen in 29.4. Knowing that these three scenes were taken in the same place enables us to strip away the smoke and reveal what the troops are advancing towards. The general terrain fits well with the south end of the training area and a low flat-topped feature is visible in the distance at a slightly higher elevation. We suggest that this is the trench from which the men emerge in the previous shot. Although we cannot be sure in which order the two scenes were shot, it seems probable that the men advanced into the smoke and kept going until they were stopped. They then turned round and were filmed going back the other way. This explains the smoke, presumably produced for a contrasting backdrop, which comes from different directions in the two shots. In shot 29.1 one can see smoke on the right of the shot, probably to beef up the effect of the shells which are falling.

Three separate sequences of shell fire which are not front-line footage appear in the film, namely 17.3–6, 27.1 and 29.1. An additional set of screen grabs appears in *Sir Douglas Haig's great push*, which are from a sequence no longer in the IWM print but still extant in the series *Our Empire's fight for freedom*. These were taken in the same place as shots 17.3–6 but not at the same time. Shots 17.3–6 follow two shots of a 9.2-inch howitzer near Bayencourt and convey the weight of fire landing on the German positions. Shots 17.3 and 17.5 were taken from the same position, while the camera has been moved to the left to take shots 17.4 and 17.6. The wire has been augmented considerably in 17.3 and 17.5, and in 17.6 a reel of wire can be seen on the left of the screen together with a shovel. The screen grabs show two additional phases; the order these were shot in is impossible to determine but one has a coat hung on a post in front of the trench and a wooden support propped up against another post on the right-hand

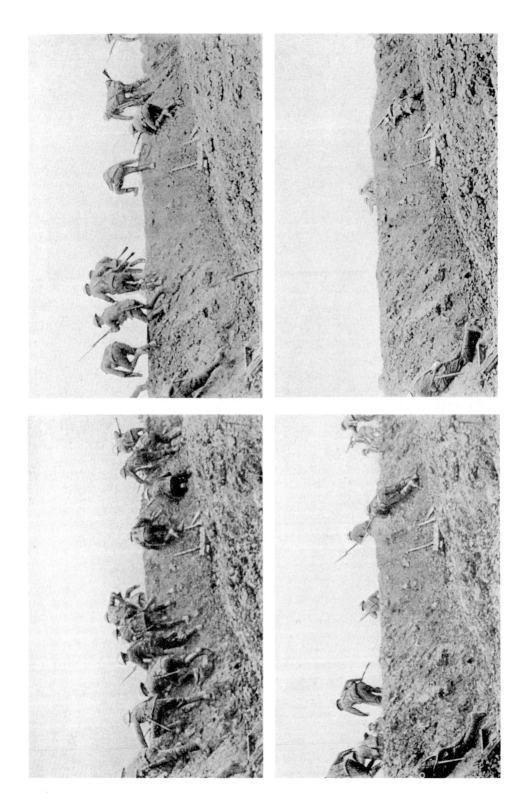

*(Opposite) Grabs from shot 31.1 showing the officer with no anti-gas protection and the men without all the equipment seen on front-line soldiers elsewhere in the film. Compare them with the men of 2 Royal Warwickshire Regiment shown in shot 33.1 (see p. 124). The weight carried by British infantry on 1 July 1916 is perhaps overemphasised as a cause of failure. What is not so clearly understood is that the attackers had to carry everything necessary to fight their way into the enemy trenches, kill the garrison and consolidate the objective against counter-attack. The men in this footage are not equipped for this task. The 'dead' soldiers are at bottom right. (DH79)*

*Note the wire support to the left of the shot which also appears in 27.1 and 29.4. One 'casualty' has already fallen into the wire. (IWM Q70168)*

side of the shot; another grab does not have the coat although the post is in the same position. It is difficult to link this location to the other two shots, 27.1 and 29.1, but the appearance of a wood and some isolated trees on the horizon suggest that it may be somewhat further north on the training area and nearer the village of Ligny-St-Flochel.

Shot 27.1 follows a series of shots of 15-inch howitzers. Again it is a demonstration of the power of British artillery. In this case the wire supports and the tree stump link

*A grab of shot 29.4. The low flat-topped feature on the horizon to the left of the shell burst may be the trench from which shot 31.1 was filmed. The same wire support appears in the centre and the wire is considerably thicker than that seen in 31.2 (the second 'over the top' scene). The sandbags in the foreground have also been increased and on the far right what appears to be additional smoke is starting to spread. (DH69)*

these two shots to the second 'over the top' sequence and enable us to see that location without the smoke. This location appears again in shot 29.4 which follows the explosion of the Hawthorn mine and is probably also intended to lead up to the dramatic sequences of the men going over the top. This filming was not without risk as the barbed wire can be seen to be disturbed by fragments from the explosions.

The vast proportion of the film was shot on the Somme in the front line. Some scenes are not quite what the captions claim they are but we can now say that only about one minute and twelve seconds in a film lasting one hour and fourteen minutes was faked. This was almost certainly because suitable footage could not be taken, rather than through any desire to mislead the audience or avoid danger.

*One of four grabs showing shelling from* Sir Douglas Haig's great push *which do not appear in the film. These survive in* Our Empire's fight for freedom *(IWM Film and Video Archive 440/6).* (DH69)

*This grab from shot 17.6, often captioned as being genuine, was filmed before the wire was thickened.* (IWM Q79487)

# CHAPTER ELEVEN

# THE EDITING AND RELEASE
# OF THE FILM

On 10 July 1916 Brigadier-General Charteris wrote to the War Office:

> I have the honour to inform you that 8,000 feet of cinema film illustrating the present British offensive has been taken by the official operators . . . The films have been sent for development and the preparation of a print. The print, it is anticipated, will be ready in a few days and will then be arranged into sections with appropriate titles, by the officer in charge of the operators, who will go to London for the purpose. It is hoped that the War Office will arrange for the issue of some sections of the films at the earliest possible date, superseding the films which the Topical War Film Committee have in hand for weekly issue. Sections aggregated to at least 2,000 feet should be issued at once. These films should be most useful for propaganda in neutral countries and especially in the United States of America.[1]

Charteris's letter clearly shows the initial thinking which was to produce a series of newsreels, differing from the previous ones only in length and perhaps quality.

The editing of the film and the uncertainty of Malins' part in it has been alluded to earlier. The film was viewed in negative on 12 July and it was presumably at that point that editing began. This job was assigned to Charles Urban, who was known in the film industry both for the speed of his editing and for his habit of smoking a cigar while working with inflammable nitrate film. He claimed that the cigar helped him to think. Urban also asserted that he was responsible for the proposal that the Somme footage should be issued as a 5,000 foot feature film rather than in shorter parts. Brooke Wilkinson remembered that after the showing on 12 July 'the committee generally agreed that it would be calamitous if they were issued in short sections'. As this arrangement was not compatible with the original agreement there were a number of meetings with the War Office before they were persuaded.[2] On 19 July Lord Newton announced that Faunthorpe had the required 5,000 feet and that the captions were being put in prior to the edited print being taken to GHQ for censorship and probable issue about 1 August. The same day Newton had written to the British Ambassador in Paris, Lord Bertie, briefing him on progress and suggesting the film should be shown in France as soon as possible.[3] On 31 July, however, Charteris was informed by the Foreign Office that the film would not be ready until the next week. It had been shown at the GHQ theatre in Montreuil to an audience including Sir Henry Rawlinson, who had commanded 4 Army on the Somme. Despite his reservations about the showing of dead soldiers there was little cutting and the delay was to do with alterations to the captions which had to be 'reprinted, rephotographed and reinserted', a process that might account for the muddled numbering of some captions in the existing running order. The altered print was viewed by Faunthorpe on 31 July. By 5 August there were fifteen positive copies in existence and more were being produced as fast as possible.[4]

The film was shown to David Lloyd George on 2 August 1916 and there was a limited trade showing on the evening of Monday, 7 August 1916 in Jury's showrooms, only a few hours after the film had been finally approved. Impressions were favourable from the start: 'we can never remember in all our long experience, to have seen any picture which, for power of appeal and intense gripping interest, comes within measurable distance of this wonderful kinematographic record'.[5] The reviewer urged every member of the trade to attend the special show the following Thursday. This was the first major exhibition and was at Distin Maddick's Scala Theatre in Fitzroy Square in London at 11.30pm on 10 August. This performance, which was presented by William Jury, included the reading of a stirring address by David Lloyd George, a special booklet and a half hour wait in sweltering heat for the film to start. It was described by the *Bioscope* as 'one of the most distinguished functions of the kind yet held in connection with the cinematograph industry' and was attended by members of the General Staff among others.[6] *The Times* of the following day reported that 'in years to come, when historians wish to know the conditions under which the great offensive was launched, they will only have to send for these films and a complete idea of the situation will be revealed before their eyes'. The correspondent also expressed the hope that copies would be preserved in the national archives.[7]

The film opened in London on 21 August 1916 and was exhibited initially in thirty-four cinemas. According to Joseph Brooke Wilkinson, *The Battle of the Somme* was a phenomenal success: 'On the evening of its release in London, I went with Jury and Malins to some of the cinemas where the film was being shown. When we arrived at the Finsbury Park Rink, we realised how great the success of the film was going to be. We had some difficulty in getting into the cinema, the excitement and enthusiasm was tremendous.'[8]

The reception of *The Battle of the Somme* and its success as a propaganda weapon are beyond the scope of this study and have been explored by other authors. Our aim has been to look at the film as an historical document and we have demonstrated that much of the footage can be fixed in time and space using a variety of techniques, some of which have not been previously applied to the study of documentary film. Although fragments are often used out of context as 'stock' footage, *The Battle of the Somme* is in fact a record of individuals with names and histories. All of them are now dead but their pain, fear, courage and humanity live on in these grey images and are perhaps more real because we now know who some of them were, when they were filmed, what they were saying and what happened to them. It is certain that the surviving print is not identical to the one seen by the audience in August 1916 but we have been able to make an important contribution to recovering some of the missing footage. The bravery and skill of the two cameramen, Geoffrey Malins and 'Mac' McDowell, have been obscured over the years by the accusations of faking. After careful study of the evidence it is certain that a very small proportion of the film can be said truly to have been faked, and we are able to say where and how this was done even if we cannot exactly fix when. It was done for technical reasons rather than as part of any cynical and sinister attempt to mislead the British public about the scale of losses on the first day of the battle. Another contentious element that we have dealt with is the assertion that Malins deliberately included much of his own footage rather than use McDowell's. Again we argue against deliberate manipulation and suggest that poor record-keeping and confusion offer a more likely explanation. Our analysis indicates that both cameramen contributed about the same amount of footage to the finished film. Geoffrey Malins is certainly a controversial figure in the history of British film making and, by virtue of having left a fuller record of his activities, has tended to occupy centre stage in previous studies of *The Battle of the Somme*. We hope that our examination of McDowell's filming has redressed the balance somewhat and restored his reputation as a combat cameraman.

Finally, to return to our original purpose, which was to treat the film as history rather than as propaganda; what we can see on the screen is the first true test of Britain's citizen army. Although none of the men in the film knew it, and many of them did not live to see it, victory was two-and-a-half years away. *The Battle of the Somme* is a fitting reminder of the horrors of war and stands as a fine memorial to the bravery, humour and determination of those who in 1916 had only just set out on that long, long trail.

# TABULATION OF SHOTS IN
# *THE BATTLE OF THE SOMME*

This list gives our estimation of the footage shot by Malins and McDowell based upon the evidence set out in the text. Material wrongly credited is given in brackets after the symbol for the correct cameraman. Some material is uncredited in the dope sheet but we have assigned it to one or other cameraman.

Note that footage and the timings of the video and DVD releases of the film vary slightly. The timings quoted in the table are those of the DVD version released in 2008.

**Abbreviations**

M – Malins
MD – McDowell
U – Uncredited
* – location marked on maps
DH – *Sir Douglas Haig's great push*

| Caption or shot | Time | Caption, place and date | Related shots and stills | Credit | Page |
|---|---|---|---|---|---|
| | 0.00.01–0.00.08 | From the Film and Video Archive of the Imperial War Museum | ------- | ------- | ------- |
| | 0.00.09–0.00.20 | United Nations Educational Scientific and Cultural Organization. Inscribed on UNESCO'S 'Memory of the World Register' – 29th July 2005. | ------- | ------- | ------- |
| | 0.00.21–0.00.25 | Imperial War Museum Official Film. Crown Copyright Reserved. | -------- | ------- | ------- |

| Caption or shot | Time | Caption, place and date | Related shots and stills | Credit | Page |
|---|---|---|---|---|---|
| | 0.00.26–0.00.32 | Battle of the Somme. Official Pictures of the British Army in France. | ------- | ------- | ------- |
| | 0.00.33–0.00.39 | Taken by permission of the War Office by the British Topical Films Committee for War Films. | ------- | ------- | ------- |
| Caption 3 | 0.00.40–0.00.53 | The Battle of the Somme. Part I. | ------- | ------- | ------- |
| Caption 4 | 0.00.54–0.01.11 | Preparatory action June 25 to 30th showing the activities before Fricourt-Mametz. Similar action took place along the entire British front in Picardy. | ------- | ------- | ------- |
| Caption 5 | 0.01.12–0.01.21 | A division waiting to move forward. June 30th. | ------- | ------- | ------- |
| 5.1–3 | 0.01.22–0.01.59 | Not located. 30/6/1916? | 10.3. DH19. Q726, Q737, Q738, Q748. | Mi (MD) | 53–5 |
| Caption 6 | 0.02.00–0.02.17 | Scenes at Bray. Platoons of the Buffs, Bedfords, Suffolks and a battalion of Royal Welsh Fusiliers moving up on the evening before the attack. | ------- | ------- | ------- |
| 6.1 | 0.02.18–0.02.29 | Bray-sur-Somme. 30/6/1916. | DH20. | MD (M) | *68–72, 156 |
| 6.2 | 0.02.30–0.02.48 | Bray-sur-Somme. 30/6/1916. | 6.3. DH20. Q79478. | MD (M) | *68–72, 156 |
| 6.3 | 0.02.49–0.03.00 | Bray-sur-Somme. 30/6/1916. | 6.2. Q79478. | MD (M) | *68–72, 156 |
| 6.4–5 | 0.03.01–0.03.37 | Not located. 30/6/1916? | DH21. Q79479–79481. | MD (M) | 72–3 |
| Caption 7 | 0.03.38–0.04.00 | Industrious French peasants continue their activities just outside the firing line. Care of artillery horses. The mascot of the Royal Field Artillery caught in France. | ------- | ------- | ------- |
| 7.1 | 0.04.01–0.04.11 | North of Bray-sur-Somme. 28/6/1916? | DH20. | MD (M) | *61–2 |

| Caption or shot | Time | Caption, place and date | Related shots and stills | Credit | Page |
|---|---|---|---|---|---|
| 9.3 | 0.06.54–0.06.57 | Acheux. 27/6/1916. | 8.2–3, 9.2, 15.1–3. DH22, DH24, DH26, DH32, DH46, DH48. Q727, Q735, Q747, Q749. | M | *33–5 |
| 9.4–5 | 0.06.58–0.07.42 | Not located. | DH27, DH30. | M | *35 |
| Caption 10 | 0.07.43–0.07.59 | A Divisional General addressing the Lancashire Fusiliers and Royal Fusiliers. A battalion of the Hampshires moving up to the attack. | | | ----- |
| 10.1–2 | 0.08.00–0.08.13 | Mailly-Maillet. 29/6/1916. | No stills. | M | *56–7 |
| 10.3–4 | 0.08.14–0.08.27 | Not located. 29/6/1916? | 5.1–3. Q728, Q738. | M | 53–5 |
| 10.5 | 0.08.28–0.08.48 | Louvencourt. 27/6/1916. | 10.6, 22.1–2, 61.1. DH31, DH58, DH162. Q716–719, Q740, Q1459, Q79482, IWM FLM 1649. | M | *26–31 |
| 10.6 | 0.08.49–0.09.02 | Louvencourt. 27/6/1916. | 10.5, 22.1–2, 61.1. DH31, DH58, DH162. Q716–719, Q79482, IWM FLM 1649. | M | *26–31 |
| Caption 11 | 0.09.03–0.09.13 | Meanwhile the 4.7-inch guns were giving the enemy no rest. | | | ----- |
| 11.1–6 | 0.09.14–0.09.49 | Not located. North of Albert. 29/6/1916? | DH28, DH33. Q79483. | M | 57 |
| Caption 12 | 0.09.50–0.10.00 | 6-inch howitzers in action shelling the German front line trenches of Mametz. | | | ----- |
| 12.1–2 | 0.10.01–0.10.14 | Bécordel. 29/6/1916? | DH32, DH35. | MD | *61–3 |
| 12.3–8 | 0.10.15–0.11.01 | East of Mansel Copse. 29–30/6/1916? | DH39. | MD | *59, 64–5, |

| | | | | | |
|---|---|---|---|---|---|
| Caption 13 | 0.11.02–0.11.16 | The vicious bark of the Canadian 60-pounders adds to the din of gunfire. Shrapnel bursting over the trenches keeps the Germans astir. | | | |
| 13.1–3 | 0.11.17–0.12.06 | Near Meaulte? 27–29/6/1916? | DH39. IWM FLM 1651. MD? | | 43, 61 |
| 13.4 | 0.12.07–0.12.50 | North of Auchonvillers. 30/6/1916? | 30.4. DH74, DH80–81. Q79484, Q79496–79497. | M | *41–6 |
| Caption 14 | 0.12.51–0.13.06 | Meanwhile more troops are started for the trenches. London Scottish and East Yorkshires. Manchesters' church service. | | | |
| 14.1–2 | 0.13.07–0.13.29 | Pas en Artois. 27/6/1916? | DH40. Q790–793. | M (MD) | *16–21 |
| 14.3 | 0.13.30–0.14.11 | Near Vauchelles? 26/6/1916? | DH44–45. Q724, Q743, IWM FLM 1557. M (MD) | | 23–4 |
| 14.4 | 0.14.12–0.14.31 | Bois des Tailles, east of Morlancourt. 28/6/1916? | DH44. Q79485. | MD | *74 |
| Caption 15 | 0.14.32–0.14.42 | Supply of 'plum puddings'. These bombs are most effective in smashing the enemy's barbed wire entanglements. | | | |
| 15.1–3 | 0.14.43–0.15.23 | Acheux. 29/6/1916. | 8.2–3, 9.2–3. DH46, DH48. | M | *33–5 |
| Caption 16 | 0.15.24–0.15.31 | Firing 'plum puddings' from trench mortars. | | | |
| 16.1–2 | 0.15.32–0.16.18 | Lanwick Street Trench, White City. 29/6/1916. | DH47. Q79486, IWM FLM 1653. | M | *49–52 |
| Caption 17 | 0.16.19–0.16.30 | Bombarding the Germans with 9.2-inch howitzers. The shells tearing up the enemy's deep dugouts. | | | |
| 17.1–2 | 0.16.31–0.17.24 | West of Bayencourt. 27/6/1916? | DH49. | M | *31–2, 167 |

| Caption or shot | Time | Caption, place and date | Related shots and stills | Credit | Page |
|---|---|---|---|---|---|
| 17.3–6 | 0.17.25–0.17.38 | Third Army Mortar School, Ligny-St-Flochel. 7/1916. | 27.1, 29.4 and 31.2. DH69. Q784–785, Q787–788, Q79487. Additional footage in Our Empire's fight for freedom (IWM Film and Video Archive 440/6). | M? | *163–71 |
| | | | | | ------ |
| | 0.17.39–0.17.48 | End of Part One. | ------ | ------ | ------ |
| Caption 3 | 0.17.49–0.17.55 | The Battle of the Somme. Part 2. | ------ | ------ | ------ |
| Caption 18 | 0.17.56–0.18.00 | The Royal Warwickshires having a meal in camp on the evening before the great advance. | ------ | ------ | ------ |
| 18.1–3 | 0.18.01–0.19.03 | Bois des Tailles. 28–30/6/1916. | DH 55–56. Q79488. | MD | *66–8 |
| 18.4 | 0.19.04–0.19.18 | Scene from The Battle of the Ancre and the Advance of the Tanks, Part 2. | ------ | ------ | 67 |
| 18.5–6 | 0.19.19–0.19.40 | Bois des Tailles. 28–30/6/1916. | DH55–56. Q79488. | MD | *66–8 |
| Caption 19 | 0.19.41–0.19.50 | High explosive shells fired by the 12-inch howitzers created havoc in the enemy's lines. | ------ | ------ | ------ |
| 19.1 | 0.19.51–0.20.07 | Humbercamps? 26–27/6/1916? | DH53–54. Q40, Q43, Q876. | M | 25 |
| 19.3–5 | 0.20.08–0.21.02 | Humbercamps? 26–27/6/1916? | DH53–54. Q40, Q43, Q876. | M | 25 |
| [Caption 20] | ? | Continuous shell fire for five days over Beaumont Hamel. | ------ | ------ | ------ |
| 20.1? | ? | Shelling of Beaumont Hamel filmed from British front line near White City. 28/6/1916. | DH57. No longer in the surviving print but some footage exists in Our Empire's fight for freedom (IWM Film and Video | | |

| | | | | M | *35–7, 91 |
|---|---|---|---|---|---|
| Caption 21 | 0.21.03–0.21.08 | A further moving up of troops. A new battalion of the Royal Warwickshires resting on their way to the trenches. | ------- | M | ------- |
| 21.1 | 0.21.09–0.21.43 | Not located. 28–30/6/1916. | DH57–58. IWM FLM 1658. Additional footage in *The Holmes Lecture Film* (IWM Film and Video Archive 468/2). | MD | 74–6 |
| Caption 22 | 0.21.44–0.21.48 | A battalion of the Worcesters fixing wire cutters to their rifles for forcing the German barbed wire entanglements. | ------- | | ------- |
| 22.1–2 | 0.21.49–0.22.34 | Louvencourt. 27/6/1916. | 10.5–6, 61.1. DH58. Q716–719. | M | *26–31 |
| Caption 23 | 0.22.35–0.22.40 | Thousands of 'flying pigs' were fired by 9.45-inch trench mortars to smash up the enemy's trenches and dugouts. | | | |
| 23.1–6 | 0.22.41–0.23.21 | Hawthorn Ridge. 29/6/1916. | DH62–63. | M | 52 |
| Caption 24 | 0.23.22–0.23.29 | A field battery brought up across the captured German trenches, in action within 2 hours of the Germans retiring. Two dumb victims. Horses killed in bringing the battery up. | | | |
| 24.1–4 | 0.23.30–0.24.02 | East of Mametz? 2/7/1916? | DH61. | MD | *132–3 |
| Caption 25 | 0.24.03–0.24.09 | Operating the 15-inch howitzer ('Grandmother') manned by the Royal Marine Artillery. Firing shells weighing 1,400 pounds each. | ------- | | ------- |

| Caption or shot | Time | Caption, place and date | Related shots and stills | Credit | Page |
|---|---|---|---|---|---|
| 25.1–2 | 0.24.10–0.24.25 | Not located. 27/6/1916? | 25.3–14, 26.1–2. DH65–68. Q31–33, Q35, Q37, Q876–879, Q79489. | M | 38–41 |
| 25.3–14 | 0.24.26–0.25.43 | South of Mailly-Maillet. 28/6/1916. | 25.1–2, 26.1–2. DH 65–68. Q31–33, Q35, Q37, Q876–879, Q79489. | M | *38–41, 169 |
| Caption 26 | 0.25.35–0.25.46 | Terrific bombardment of the German trenches. | ------ | ------ | ------ |
| 26.1–2 | 0.25.47–0.26.00 | South of Mailly-Maillet. 28/6/1916. | 25.1–14. DH65. Q31–33, Q35, Q37, Q876–879, Q79489. | M | *38–41, 169 |
| Caption 27 | 0.26.01–0.26.04 | The morning of the attack. July 1st 1916. | ------ | ------ | ------ |
| 27.1 | 0.26.05–0.26.29 | Third Army Mortar School, Ligny-St-Flochel. 7/1916. | 17.3–6, 29.4, 31.2. DH69. Q784–785, Q787–788, Q79487. | M? | *163–71 |
| Caption 28 | 0.26.30–0.26.37 | A Lancashire battalion awaiting instructions, fixing bayonets and passing through communication trenches to the front line. Bombers taking up supplies. | ------ | ------ | ------ |
| 28.1 | 0.26.38–0.26.58 | White City. 30/6/1916. | DH70. Q796. | M | *77–8, 86–7 |
| 28.2–4 | 0.26.59–0.27.53 | White City. 30/6/1916. | DH71. Q744, Q79490–79491. | M | *78–84, 105 |
| Caption 29 | 0.27.54–0.28.02 | Just before the attack. Blowing up enemy trenches by a huge mine. Royal Engineers rushing off to wire | | | |

the crater for occupation by the advancing troops.

| | | | | |
|---|---|---|---|---|
| 29.1 | 0.28.03–0.28.16 | White City. 30/6/1916. | DH54, DH77. Q731. M | *84, 105 |
| 29.2–3 | 0.28.17–0.28.31 | White City. 1/7/1916. | DH75. Q22, Q754, Q756, Q50324–50325. M. | *88–91 |
| 29.4 | 0.28.32–0.28.45 | Third Army Mortar School, Ligny-St.-Flochel. 7/1916. | 17.3–6, 27.1, 31.2. DH69. Q787–788, Q79487. Additional footage in *Our Empire's fight for freedom* (IWM Film and Video Archive 440/6). M | 163–71 |
| | | Footage of La Boisselle mine crater. | In the video release this footage follows shot 29.4 and is repeated at shots 51.3–4. In the DVD version it is only shown as shots 51.3–4. See entry for shots 51.3–4 for details. M | |
| Caption 30 | 0.28.46.–0.28.49 | Setting up machine guns. Firing from top of trench parapet. Shrapnel bursting over German front line trenches. | ------- | ------ |
| 30.1 | 0.28.50–0.28.55 | North of Auchonvillers? 30/6/1916? | DH77. | M (MD) | 41 |
| 30.2–4 | 0.28.56–0.29.51 | North of Auchonvillers. 30/6/1916? | 13.4. DH74, DH80–81. Q79484, Q79496–79497. | M (MD) | *41–6 |
| | 0.29.52–0.30.01 | End of Part Two. | | |
| Caption 3 | 0.30.02–0.30.07 | The Battle of the Somme. Part 3. | ------- | ------ |

| Caption or shot | Time | Caption, place and date | Related shots and stills | Credit | Page |
|---|---|---|---|---|---|
| Caption 31 | 0.30.08–0.30.18 | The attack. At a signal, along the entire 16 mile front, the British troops leaped over the trench parapets, and advanced towards the German trenches, under the heavy fire of the enemy. | ------- | ------- | |
| 31.1 | 0.30.19–0.30.32 | Third Army Mortar School, Ligny-St.-Flochel. 7/1916. | 31.2. DH78–79. Q65405–65407, Q70164–70166, Q70693A, Q70694– 70695, Q79498–79499, Q112291–112292. | M? | *163–71 |
| 31.2 | 0.30.33–0.30.40 | Third Army Mortar School, Ligny-St.-Flochel. 7/16. | 27.1, 31.1. DH82. Q65408–65409, Q70167–70169, Q70693, Q70696– 70699, Q75500. IWM FILM 1654. | M? | *163–71 |
| 31.3–4 | 0.30.41–0.31.30 | White City. 1/7/1916. | Q745, Q750, Q755, Q757. | M | *79, 88–95, 166 |
| Caption 32 | 0.31.31–0.31.38 | A sunken road in 'no-man's-land' occupied by the Lancashire Fusiliers (20 minutes after this picture was taken these men came under heavy machine gun fire). | ------- | ------- | ------- |
| 32.1–2 | 0.31.39–0.32.03 | Sunken Lane, Beaumont Hamel. 1/7/1916. | DH82. IWM FLM 1672–1673. | M | *86–8 |
| 32.3–4 | 0.32.04–0.32.17 | Sunken Lane, Beaumont Hamel. 1/7/1916. | DH82. IWM FLM 1672–1673. | M | *86–8 |
| 32.5 | 0.32.18–0.32.30 | Sunken Lane, Beaumont Hamel. 1/7/1916. | DH82. IWM FLM 1672–1673 | M | *86–8 |

| | | | | | |
|---|---|---|---|---|---|
| Caption 33 | 0.32.31–0.32.34 | **Warwickshires advancing up a captured trench to relieve the Queens in the front line.** | ------- | ------- | ------- |
| 33.1 | 0.32.35–0.32.56 | Probably east of Mametz. 1–4/7/1916. | DH82. Additional footage in *The Holmes Lecture Film* (IWM Film and Video Archive 468/3). | MD | 124, 169 |
| Caption 34 | 0.32.57–0.33.04 | **British Tommies rescuing a comrade under shell fire.** (This man died 30 minutes after reaching the trenches.) **Conveying wounded by wheeled stretcher.** | ------- | ------- | ------- |
| 34.1 | 0.33.05–0.33.17 | Tenderloin, White City. 1/7/1916. | 34.2–3. DH86. Q752–753, Q79501. | M | *79, 91–2, 96–9 |
| 34.2 | 0.33.18–0.33.24 | Tenderloin, White City. 1/7/1916. | 34.1, 34.3. DH89. Q752–753, Q79501. | M | *96–9 |
| 34.3 | 0.33.25–0.33.36 | Tenderloin, White City. 1/7/1916. | 34.1–2. DH86. Q752–753, Q79501. | M | *96–9 |
| 34.4 | 0.33.37–0.33.44 | Albert to Bapaume Road near Bapaume Post Cemetery. 3/7/1916? | 38.1–4. DH86. | M | *144–7 |
| Caption 35 | 0.33.45–0.34.00 | **Bringing in the wounded.** | ------- | ------- | ------- |
| 35.1 | 0.34.01–0.34.11 | White City. 30/6/1916. | DH90. Q65410, Q101064. | M | *85 |
| 35.2–3 | 0.34.12–0.34.35 | Sunken Road, north-east of Auchonvillers. 30/6/1916? | DH93–94. Q79502. | M | *47–9 |
| 35.4 | 0.34.36–0.34.55 | East of Mametz? 1/7/1916. | 36.7. DH94. Q65411–65412, IWM FLM 1660. | MD (M) | 127–9 |

| Caption or shot | Time | Caption, place and date | Related shots and stills | Credit | Page |
|---|---|---|---|---|---|
| 35.5–7 | 0.34.56–0.35.47 | Tenderloin, White City. 1/7/1916. | DH91, DH105. Q739, Q65414. | M | *56, 100–2 |
| 35.8 | 0.35.48–0.35.57 | West of Carnoy? 1/7/1916? | 36.1–11, 47.1. DH96. | MD | 125–7 |
| Caption 36 | 0.35.58–0.36.03 | A Lancashire battalion which has been relieved after a successful attack returns with prisoners. Friend and foe help each other. | ------- | ------- | ------- |
| 36.1–5 | 0.36.04–0.37.24 | Between Mametz and Carnoy. 1/7/1916. | 35.8, 36.6–11, 47.1. DH96. | MD (M) | *125–7 |
| 36.6–10 | 0.37.25–0.38.11 | Between Mametz and Carnoy. 1/7/1916. | 35.8, 36.1–5, 36.11, 47.1. DH95. | MD (M) | *125–7 |
| 36.11 | 0.38.12–0.38.26 | Between Mametz and Carnoy. 1/7/1916 | 35.8, 36.1–10, 47.1. DH95. | MD (M) | *125–7 |
| Caption 37 | 0.38.27–0.38.35 | Royal Field Artillery moving up during battle over ground where the Gordons' and Devons' dead are lying after a glorious and successful charge on the ridge near Mametz. | | | |
| Caption 37a | 0.38.36–0.38.41 | These two batteries advanced under fire to a position beyond Mametz and were fortunate in having no casualties. | ------- | ------- | ------- |
| 37.1 | 0.38.42–0.39.03 | Valley north of Mansel Copse. 2/7/1916. | 37.2–3. DH100. Q79503 | MD | *34, 129–31 |
| 37.2–3 | 0.39.04–0.39.50 | Valley north of Mansel Copse. 2/7/1916. | 37.1. DH100. Q79503. | MD | *34, 129–31 |
| Caption 38 | 0.39.51–0.39.53 | One of five unsuccessful counter-attacks at La Boisselle. | ------- | ------- | ------- |
| 38.1–2 | 0.39.54–0.40.42 | East of Albert to Bapaume Road. 3/7/1916? | 34.4. DH114. | M | *144–7 |

| | | | | | |
|---|---|---|---|---|---|
| 38.3–4 | 0.40.43–0.40.56 | Albert to Bapaume Road. 3/7/1916? | 34.4. Q770, Q774. | M | *144–7 |
| Caption 39 | 0.40.57–0.41.03 | Scene in 'Dantzig Alley' captured and held by a battalion of the Manchesters. A captured trench mortar. | ------- | ------- | ------- |
| 39.1 | 0.41.04–0.41.16 | East end of Mametz. 2/7/1916? | DH112–113. Q65415–65416. | MD | *137–9 |
| 39.2 | 0.41.17–0.41.27 | Mametz? 2/7/1916? | DH114. | MD | 137–9 |
| Caption 40 | 0.41.28–0.41.41 | Activity at Minden Post, while the battle raged furiously. Arrival of wounded Tommies. The front line trenches are just over the crest about 200 yards away. | | | |
| 40.1 | 0.41.42–0.42.10 | Minden Post. 1/7/1916. | DH112–113. Q65417–65418. | MD | *107–9 |
| 40.2 | 0.42.11–0.42.13 | Minden Post. 1/7/1916. | No stills. | MD | *107–9 |
| Caption 41 | 0.42.14–0.42.26 | Stretcher cases for ambulance. Wounded awaiting attention at Minden Post. Showing how quickly the wounded are attended to. | ------- | ------- | ------- |
| 41.1 | 0.42.27–0.42.53 | Main road above Minden Post. 1/7/1916. | DH117. | MD | *109–13 |
| 41.2 | 0.42.54–0.43.08 | Minden Post. 1/7/1916 | DH117. Q65419. | MD | *109–13 |
| 41.3 | 0.43.09–0.43.29 | Minden Post. 1/7/1916. | Q65420, Q79504. | MD | *109–13 |
| 41.4 | 0.43.30–0.43.39 | Minden Post. 1/7/1916. | No stills. | MD | *109–13 |
| | 0.43.49–0.43.49 | End of Part Three. | | | |
| Caption 42X | 0.43.50–0.43.57 | The Battle of the Somme. Part 4. | ------- | ------- | ------- |
| Caption 42 | 0.43.58–0.44.05 | British wounded and nerve-shattered German prisoners arriving. Officer giving drink, and Tommies offering cigarettes to German prisoners. | ------- | ------- | ------- |
| 42.1 | 0.44.06–0.44.14 | Minden Post. 1/7/1916. | Q79506. | MD (M) | *107, 115–20 |

| Caption or shot | Time | Caption, place and date | Related shots and stills | Credit | Page |
|---|---|---|---|---|---|
| 42.2–3 | 0.44.15–0.45.00 | Minden Post. 1/7/1916 | Q65434–65435, Q79507–79508. | MD (M) | *107, 115–20 |
| 42.4–5 | 0.45.01–0.45.37 | Track south of Minden Post. 1/7/1916. | 34[43].1. DH121. Q79509–79510. | MD (M) | *107, 120–1 |
| Caption 34 – should be 43 | 0.45.38–0.45.43 | Taking papers from and handing identification books back to prisoners. More captures. | ------- | ------- | ------- |
| 34[43].1 | 0.45.44–0.45.53 | Track south of Minden Post. 1/7/1916 | 42.4–5. DH121. Q65436–65437. | MD (M) | *107, 120–1 |
| 34[43]2–5 | 0.45.54–0.47.53 | Minden Post.1/7/1916. | DH120. Q79511–79513. | MD (M) | *107, 115–21 |
| Caption 44 | 0.47.54–0.48.04 | Scenes at the dressing station for slightly wounded at Minden Post. In background appears a battalion of Manchester Pioneers waiting to go down to the German trenches when captured. | ------- | ------- | ------- |
| 44.1–3 | 0.48.05–0.48.45 | Minden Post. 1/7/1916 | DH120. Q65435. | MD | *113–15 |
| 44.4–7 | 0.48.46–0.50.08 | Minden Post. 1/7/1916. | DH118–119. Q65439–65440, Q79514. | MD | *113–15 |
| Caption 45 | 0.50.09–0.50.22 | German curtain fire just outside Minden Post. Part of the British fire trench wrecked by German high explosive shells a few minutes before this picture was taken. | ------- | ------- | ------- |
| 45.1–2 | 0.50.23–0.51.26 | North-west of Minden Post. 1/7/1916. | Q79515. | MD | *123, |

| | | | | MD | 123 |
|---|---|---|---|---|---|
| 45.3 | 0.51.27–0.51.40 | Minden Avenue? 1/7/1916? | Q79505. | MD | 123 |
| Caption 46 | 0.51.41–0.51.45 | **Clearing the battlefield of snipers and hidden machine guns. Routing Germans from dugouts.** | ------ | ------ | ------ |
| 46.1 | 0.51.46–0.52.05 | West of Montauban. 5–6/7/1916? | 46.2. DH137. | M | *156–7 |
| 46.2 | 0.52.06–0.52.26 | West of Montauban. 5–6/7/1916? | 46.1. DH137. Q79516, IWM FLM 1656. | M | *156–7 |
| Caption 47 | 0.52.27–0.52.35 | **Battle police rounding up more prisoners and wounded in 'no-man's-land'. Prisoners in compound awaiting transportation.** | ------ | ------ | ------ |
| 47.1 | 0.52.36–0.53.05 | West of Carnoy. 1/7/16. | 35.8, 36.1–11. | MD (M) | *125–7 |
| 47.2–3 | 0.53.06–0.53.35 | South of Acheux. 2/7/1916. | DH158. Q732. | M | *140–3 |
| Caption 48 | 0.53.36–0.53.42 | **Effects of British shell fire on German trenches between Fricourt and Mametz. The post reaches the Devonshires during battle.** | ------ | ------ | ------ |
| 48.1 | 0.53.43–0.54.01 | South-west of Mametz? 1/7/1916. | Q79517. | MD (U) | 133 |
| 48.2 | 0.54.02–0.54.13 | South-west of Mametz? 1/7/1916. | DH141. | MD (U) | 133 |
| 48.3 | 0.54.14–0.54.30 | South-west of Mametz? 1/7/1916. | DH138. | MD (U) | 133 |
| 48.4 | 0.54.31–0.54.48 | South-west of Mametz? 1/7/1916. | DH138. | MD (U) | 133 |
| Caption 49 | 0.54.49–0.54.51 | **The toll of war. German dead on the field of battle.** | ------ | ------ | ------ |
| 49.1 | 0.54.52–0.55.02 | La Boisselle area? 3/7/1916? | 51.1–2. Q65441–65442, Q79518. | M (MD) | *149 |
| Caption 50 | 0.55.03–0.55.08 | **The Manchesters' pet dog fell with his master charging Danzig Alley.** | ------ | ------ | ------ |
| 50.1 | 0.55.09–0.55.15 | West of Mametz. 1/7/1916? | DH142. Q79519. | MD(U) | *133–7 |

| Caption or shot | Time | Caption, place and date | Related shots and stills | Credit | Page |
|---|---|---|---|---|---|
| 50.2 | 0.55.16–0.55.29 | Near Mametz? 2/7/1916? | DH143. Q65444. | MD | *133–7 |
| 50.3 | 0.55.30–0.55.38 | Near Mametz? 2/7/1916? | No stills. | MD | *133–7 |
| 50.4 | 0.55.39–0.55.55 | Near Mametz? 2/7/1916? | DH141. | MD | *133–7 |
| 50.5 | 0.55.56–0.56.04 | Near Mametz? 2/7/1916? | Q65445, Q79520. | MD | *133–7 |
| 50.6 | 0.56.05–0.56.10 | Between Carnoy and Montauban. 2/7/1916. | 50.7–9. DH143. Q65446. | MD (M) | *133–7 |
| 50.7 | 0.56.11–0.56.18 | Between Carnoy and Montauban. 2/7/1916. | 50.6, 50.8–9. DH143. | MD (M) | *133–7 |
| 50.8 | 0.56.19–0.56.35 | Between Carnoy and Montauban. 2/7/1916. | 50.6–7, 50.9. DH143. Q65447. | MD (M) | *133–7 |
| 50.9 | 0.56.36–0.56.50 | Between Carnoy and Montauban. 2/7/1916. | 50.6–8. DH143. Q79521. | MD (M) | *133–7 |
|  | 0.56.51–0.57.00 | End of Part Four. | ------ | ------ | ------ |
| Caption 3 | 0.57.01–0.57.07 | The Battle of the Somme. Part 5. | ------ | ------ | ------ |
| Caption 51 | 0.57.08–0.57.18 | The devastating effect of British shell fire. Smashed trenches and dug-outs. A mine crater 40 feet deep. |  |  |  |
| 51.1 | 0.57.19–0.57.38 | La Boisselle? 3–5/7/1916? | 49.1, 51.2–4. | M | *147–9 |
| 51.2 | 0.57.39–0.58.02 | La Boisselle? 3–5/7/1916? | 49.1, 51.1, 3–4. | M | *147–9 |
| 51.3–4 | 0.58.03–0.58.59 | La Boisselle. 3–5/7/1916. | 49.1, 51.1–3. DH145. Q79522. IWM FLM 1659. | M | *147 |
| Caption 52 | 0.59.00–0.59.16 | The battered German stronghold at Fricourt. Wrecked dugouts 20–30 feet under level of field. A labour battalion of the Duke of Cornwall's Light Infantry repairing road on day following battle. | ------ | ------ | ------ |
| 52.1 | 0.59.17–0.59.37 | Fricourt. 6/7/1916. | DH148. | M | *161–2 |
| 52.2 | 0.59.38–1.00.55 | Mametz. 5/7/1916? | 53.1–3. DH144. | M |  |

| | | | Q772–773, Q1063. | M | *153–4 |
|---|---|---|---|---|---|
| 52.3 | 1.00.56–1.01.31 | Not located. 5/7/1916? | DH142. | M | 154–5 |
| Caption 53 | | Views of the shell-shattered village of Mametz. The main street. German dugouts. | ------ | ------ | ------ |
| 53.1 | 1.01.39–1.01.56 | Mametz. 5/7/1916. | 52.2. DH146. Q772–773, Q1063. | M | *153–4 |
| 53.2 | 1.01.57–1.02.30 | Mametz. 5/7/1916. | 52.2. DH147. Q772–773, Q1063. | M | *153–4 |
| 53.3 | 1.02.31–1.02.38 | Mametz. 5/7/1916. | 52.2. DH146. Q772–773, Q1063. | M | *153–4 |
| 53.4 | 1.02.39–1.02.56 | Fricourt. 5/7/1916? | 53.5. DH166. | M | *155, 162 |
| 53.5 | 1.02.57–1.03.15 | Fricourt. 5/7/1916? | 53.4. DH148. | M | *155, 162 |
| Caption 54 | ------ | Not present. | ------ | ------ | ------ |
| Caption 55 | 1.03.16–1.03.28 | Some of the booty. German trench mortars. Battery of field artillery captured by the 7th Division near La Boisselle. | ------ | ------ | ------ |
| 55.1–2 | 1.03.29–1.04.12 | Carnoy? 5/7/1916? | DH149. | M | 150–1 |
| 55.3 | 1.04.13–1.04.35 | Carnoy? 5/7/1916? | DH150. | M. | 150–1 |
| 55.4–5 | 1.04.36–1.04.44 | Carnoy? 5/7/1916. | DH150. | M | 151–2 |
| Caption 56 | 1.04.45–1.04.53 | A welcome rest. Lancashire Fusiliers after the battle. Assembling for roll call. | ------ | ------ | ------ |
| 56.1 | 1.04.54–1.05.13 | White City. 1/7/1916. | DH151. | M (MD) | *102–3 |
| 56.2 | 1.05.14–1.05.27 | White City. 1/7/1916 | Q730. | M | *102–4 |
| 56.3 | 1.05.28–1.05.44 | Not located. Possibly valley south of Ville-sur-Ancre. 8/7/1916? | 57.1–2. DH151. | M? | 160–1 |

| Caption or shot | Time | Caption, place and date | Related shots and stills | Credit | Page |
|---|---|---|---|---|---|
| 56.4. | 1.05.45–1.06.06 | White City. 1/7/1916. | No stills. | M | *102–3 |
| 56.5 | 1.06.07–1.06.22 | White City. 1/7/1916. | Q746. | M | *104–5 |
| Caption 57 | 1.06.23–1.06.30 | **Royal Fusiliers cleaning up after the successful advance.** | ------ | ------ | ------ |
| 57.1–2 | 1.06.31–1.07.08 | Valley south of Ville-sur-Ancre. 8/7/1916? | 56.3. DH152. | M | *160–1 |
| 57.3–5 | 1.07.09–1.07.56 | Albert to Bapaume road. 7/7/1916? | 56.3. DH152–153. Q775–777, Q781, Q797–798, IWM FLM 1648. | M | *160–1 |
| Caption 58 | 1.07.57–1.08.09 | **Essex Regiment washing up at a wayside pool. Roll-call of the Seaforth Highlanders.** | ------ | ------ | ------ |
| 58.1 | 1.08.10–1.08.26 | Carnoy area? 5/7/1916. | DH153, DH251. | M | 152–3 |
| 58.2–4 | 1.08.27–1.09.04 | White City. 1/7/1916. | DH153. Q746. | M | *104–5 |
| Caption 59 | 1.09.05–1.09.11 | **Cleaning up machine guns. A cheery group of gunners and Highlanders on the battlefield.** | ------ | ------ | ------ |
| 59.1 | 1.09.12–1.09.27 | White City. 1/7/1916. | 59.2. DH154. | M | *44, 106 |
| 59.2 | 1.09.28–1.09.47 | White City. 1/7/1916. | 59.1. DH154. | M | *44, 106 |
| 59.3 | 1.09.48–1.10.04 | Valley north of Mansel Copse? 2/7/1916. | DH154. | MD | |
| Caption 60 | 1.10.05–1.10.11 | **Bringing up an 8-inch howitzer and placing it in advanced position for the next bombardment.** | ------ | ------ | ------ |
| 60.1 | 1.10.12–1.10.40 | Bécordel. 6/7/1916. | 60.2–5. DH160–161. Q794–795, Q827. | M | *157–9 |
| 60.2 | 1.10.41–1.10.48 | Bécordel. 6/7/1916. | 60.1, 61.3–5. DH160–161. Q794–795, Q827. | M | |
| 60.3 | 1.10.49–1.10.55 | Bécordel. 6/7/1916. | 60.1–2, 60.4–5. DH160–161. | M | *157–9 |

| ID | Timecode | Description | Reference | | Pages |
|---|---|---|---|---|---|
| | | | Q794–795, Q827. | M | *157–9 |
| 60.4 | 1.10.56–1.11.05 | Bécordel. 6/7/1916. | 60.1–3, 60.5. DHI60–161. Q794–795, Q827. | M | *157–9 |
| 60.5 | 1.11.06–1.11.08 | Bécordel. 6/7/1916. | 60.1–4. DHI60–161. Q794–759, Q827. | M | *157–9 |
| Caption 61 | 1.11.09–1.11.15 | Seeking further laurels. A 'sample' of the British Army (the Worcesters) off to continue the advance. | ------- | ------ | ------ |
| 61.1 | 1.11.16–1.11.38 | Louvencourt. 27/6/1916. | 10.5, 22.1–2. DHI62. Q716–719. | M | *26–31 |
| Caption 62 | 1.11.39–1.11.45 | Whilst 'others' less fortunate depart under escort for England. | ------ | ------ | ------ |
| 62.1 | 1.11.46–1.12.06 | South of Acheux. 2/7/1916. | 47.2–3. DHI58. | M | *140–3 |
| 62.2 | 1.12.07–1.12.32 | South of Acheux. 2/7/1916. | 47.2–3. DHI58. | M | *140–3 |
| 62.3 | 1.12.33–1.12.41 | South of Acheux. 2/7/1916. | 47.2–3. DHI58. | M | *140–3 |
| Caption 63 | 1.13.42–1.13.49 | The end. | ------ | ------ | ------ |
| | | Map inserted in April 1917 or later. Not included in the IWM release on DVD. | ------ | ------ | ------ |

# NOTES

## Chapter 2

1. Reeves, 1986 and 1989; Hiley.
2. INF4/2, 293; Urban Papers, 4/1, 24.
3. Lytton, 113.
4. INF4/2, 195.
5. McDowell's biography is supplied by Dr Nick Hiley; *Kinematograph and Lantern Weekly* (*KW*), 13 July 1916.

## Chapter 3

1. Enticknap; Jones. Thanks to Michael Harvey of the National Media Museum.
2. David Walsh, Head of Film Preservation at the Imperial War Museum (pers. comm.); Roger Smither (pers. comm.).
3. FO395/37 – 135744/8403; *KW*, 13 July 1916.
4. Brownlow 1979, 67.

## Chapter 4

1. Laing letter, IWM.
2. WO95/2956.
3. CWGC. *The Times*, 29 Mar. 1971.
4. WO374/20382.
5. WO95/2956; *The Times*; *Internet Movie Database*.
6. WO95/2956; WO374/64294; *The Times*, 19 Oct. 1933.
7. WO374/16186.
8. *London Scottish Regimental Gazette*, 1918, 9.
9. London Scottish Regimental Museum; CWGC; WO95/2956.
10. WO95/2357; Carver, 92–3.
11. Hall diary, NAM; WO95/2280.
12. WO95/2306.
13. WO95/2305.
14. WO95/820.
15. Malins, 131; WO95/824.
16. WO95/863; Malins, 137–8; Blumberg, 286.
17. Malins, 130–1.
18. Ibid, 126–7; Trench maps 57dSE1 and 2 *Beaumont*, editions 2B, 2C, 2D.

19. WO95/1490.
20. 119 RIR battle report.
21. Ibid.
22. Translation from Staatsarchiv 109 Bü. 44.
23. Holtz, 34–6.
24. WO95/2292; WO95/2287.
25. Malins, 148.
26. *VN*, 11.
27. WO95/2295.
28. WO95/2143.
29. Malins, 136–7; De Lisle, 64, 147–50.
30. De Lisle, 64–5; De Lisle narrative, v.2, 9; *The Times*, 14 Mar. 1952.
31. WO95/2300; Laing letter, IWM; Ashurst, 96; *Lancashire Fusiliers Annual*, 34–5.
32. Farndale, 144.

## Chapter 5

1. *KW*, 13 July 1916, 11, and *Screen* (*SC*), 7 Oct. 1916. There is discussion about the respective contributions of Malins and McDowell in Nicholas Hiley's thesis, 'Making war: the British news media and government control 1914–1916'. We are grateful for Dr Hiley's permission to quote from this work.
2. *KW*, 13 July 1916.
3. Ibid.
4. *The Times*, 5 Sept. 1916; *KW*, 13 July 1916; INF4/2, 296.
5. *SC*, 7 Oct. 1916.
6. National Archives of Canada, war diaries of 1 Canadian Heavy Battery, RG9-III-D-3; WO95/925.
7. Hogg and Thurston, 124–5.
8. Middlebrook, M. and M., 86; Committee of Imperial Defence, *Official History, France and Belgium 1916* (*OH*), vol. 1, 354.
9. *OH 1916*, vol. 1, 351–68; see also Stedman, 1997 (1).
10. WO95/1664.
11. WO95/1630.
12. Ibid.
13. *VN*, 10.
14. Middlebrook 1971, 110ff; WO95/2043.
15. Middlebrook (pers. comm.); WO95/2043.
16. *The Times*, 23 July 1917; WO339/19432; WO95/2043.
17. *KW*, 13 July 1916, 11.
18. WO95/2085.

## Chapter 6

1. Reed, 64–5 and pers. comm.
2. Swinton, 1075.

3. Hurst, 147 and pers. comm.
4. Chappell, 27; WO95/2300; LFA 2060.
5. Ashurst, 98. Thanks to the Crowood Press for permission to quote from his work.
6. *Lancashire Fusiliers Annual*, 1916, 43.
7. 119 RIR battle report.
8. Thanks to Judy Ruyzlo of Yap Films, David Pinney of Trent College, Nottingham, Jade Publications of Oldham and Ashton-under-Lyne Public Library for tracking down photographs.
9. *Gallipoli Gazette*, Spring 1964, 147.
10. LFA 2060.
11. WO95/2300.
12. WO95/2296.

# Chapter 7

1. Malins, 154–61; WO95/2300; WO95/2302.
2. *OH 1916*, vol. 1, 429–38; Sheldon 2006 (1), 65–88; Gerster, 51–4.
3. Crawford, 120.
4. WO95/2298; Barton 2005, 313.
5. Smither; *Southend-on-Sea Pictorial*, 23 Dec. 1964.
6. WO95/2300; Latter, vol. 1, 138; CAB45/137.
7. *Army List*; *The Times*; *London Gazette*; CWGC.
8. WO95/1445.
9. WO95/1483.
10. WO95/1485.

# Chapter 8

1. Chris McCarthy (pers. comm.).
2. WO95/1630.
3. WO95/1647.
4. Ibid; WO95/2296.
5. *OH 1916*, vol. 1, 368; WO95/1642.
6. Stosch, 71; Frisch, 118ff.
7. WO95/1630.
8. Cron et al; Ralph Whitehead (pers. comm.).
9. WO95/1670.
10. Ibid.
11. WO95/1668–1669.
12. Ralph Whitehead (pers. comm.).
13. *SC*, Northern Section, p. ix.
14. WO95/1643.
15. Crosse, 2–3, IWM Dept of Docs.
16. Sassoon, 62.
17. Hammerton, vol. 2, 718; WO95/1655; WO95/1656.

18. WO95/1643.
19. WO95/1655.
20. Thanks to Steve Hurst, Harold Lewis's great-nephew, for information about him. Other material comes from M. Stedman's *Manchester Pals*, P. Hart's *The Somme* and the battalion war diary at WO95/1663.
21. Dr Tal Simmons (pers. comm.); WO95/2044.
22. WO95/1668; WO95/1669.

## Chapter 9

1. Malins, 171. Gliddon 2006, 86–7.
2. Falls 1922, 59.
3. Fabeck, 44.
4. James, 21; WO95/828.
5. *OH 1916*, vol. 2, 12; Stosch, 112–16.
6. *OH 1916*, vol. 1, 375ff; Stosch, 53ff.
7. WO95/1630.
8. WO95/2043.
9. WO95/388.
10. WO95/2532; Chapman, 98.
11. WO95/517.

## Chapter 10

1. *Durham Advertiser*, 29 Sept. 1916.
2. Hiley, 618.
3. Malins, 303.
4. Brooks Carrington interview.
5. Hiley, 694; Ernest Brooks, 12 Dec. 1916.
6. Brooks Carrington interview.
7. Ibid.
8. Malins, 122.

## Chapter 11

1. FO395/37 File 103810.
2. Urban 4/1–188; INF4/2, 298–9.
3. FO395/37 File 140948.
4. FO395/37 File 157531.
5. *KW*, 10 Aug. 1916, 7.
6. *Bioscope*, 17 Aug. 1916, 579.
7. *The Times*, 11 Aug. 1916, 3.
8. INF 4/2, 299.

# BIBLIOGRAPHY

## Archive Material

**National Archives**

Cabinet Office

CAB45/137          E.W. Sheppard's narrative of 1 July 1916.

War Office

WO95/388           56 Siege Battery, Royal Garrison Artillery.
WO95/517           12 Duke of Cornwall's Light Infantry, Fourth Army.
WO95/820           VIII Corps, General Staff.
WO95/824           VIII Corps, Commander Royal Artillery.
WO95/828           1/1 Lancashire Hussars.
WO95/863           X Corps, Commander Royal Artillery.
WO95/925           XV Corps, Commander Royal Artillery.
WO95/1444–1445     4 Division, General Staff.
WO95/1478–1479     10 Infantry Brigade, 4 Division.
WO95/1483          2 Seaforth Highlanders, 4 Division.
WO95/1485          10 Infantry Brigade Machine Gun Company, 4 Division.
WO95/1490          11 Infantry Brigade, 4 Division.
WO95/1500          11 Infantry Brigade Machine Gun Company, 4 Division.
WO95/1630          7 Division, General Staff.
WO95/1642          14 Brigade, Royal Horse Artillery, 7 Division.
WO95/1643          35 Brigade, Royal Field Artillery, 7 Division.
WO95/1646          24 Manchester Regiment, 7 Division.
WO95/1647          22 Field Ambulance, 7 Division.
WO95/1655          8 Devons, 7 Division.
WO95/1656          2 Gordon Highlanders, 7 Division.
WO95/1663          20 Manchester Regiment, 7 Division.
WO95/1664          2 Royal Warwickshire Regiment, 7 Division.
WO95/1668          21 Manchester Regiment, 7 Division.
WO95/1669          22 Manchester Regiment, 7 Division.
WO95/1670          2 Queen's (Royal West Surrey Regiment), 7 Division.
WO95/2043          7 Bedfordshire Regiment, 18 Division.
WO95/2044          12 Middlesex Regiment, 18 Division.
WO95/2085          10 Royal Warwickshire Regiment, 19 Division.

| WO95/2143 | 21 Division, Trench Mortar Batteries. |
| WO95/2280 | General Staff, 29 Division. |
| WO95/2287 | 29 Division, Commander Royal Artillery. |
| WO95/2292 | 132 Howitzer Brigade, 29 Division. |
| WO95/2295 | 1/2 Monmouthshire Regiment, 29 Division. |
| WO95/2296 | 87 Field Ambulance, 29 Division. |
| WO95/2298 | 86 Infantry Brigade, 29 Division. |
| WO95/2300 | 1 Lancashire Fusiliers, 29 Division. |
| WO95/2302 | 86 Trench Mortar Battery, 29 Division. |
| WO95/2305 | 88 Infantry Brigade Machine Gun Company, 29 Division. |
| WO95/2306 | 88 Infantry Brigade, 29 Division. |
| WO95/2357 | 10 East Yorkshire Regiment, 31 Division. |
| WO95/2532 | 13 Royal Fusiliers, 37 Division. |
| WO95/2956 | 1/London Scottish, 56 Division. |
| WO339/19432 | D.H. Keep. |
| WO364/1071 | J.H. Dunbar. |
| WO374/16186 | H.A. Coxon. |
| WO374/20382 | A.G. Douglas. |
| WO374/64294 | H.C. Sparkes. |

Foreign Office
FO395/37          News Department files, 1916.

Ministry of Information
INF4/2            Joseph Brooke Wilkinson's account of wartime film, 1939.

**National Army Museum**
Diary of Lt Hall, 2 Hampshire Regiment.
**Staatsarchiv, Stuttgart**
109 Bü 44 – War diary of 121 RIR.
**Kevin Brownlow**
Transcript of interview with Bertram Brooks Carrington, 1972.
Photographs of J.B. McDowell.
**Fusiliers Museum, Bury**
LFA 2060. Operations order, C Company, 1 Lancashire Fusiliers, 1916.
**Imperial War Museum, Department of Documents**
Trench diary of Revd Ernest Courtenay Crosse. 80/22/1
**Imperial War Museum, Department of Film and Video Archive**
Ernest Brooks correspondence.
Particulars of *Battle of the Somme* film screened on 4 May 1922, including dope sheet.
Dope sheet for *The Battle of the Ancre and the Advance of the Tanks*.
Letter from David Laing to Tony Essex, 1964.

**National Archives of Canada**
RG9-III-D-3 – 1 Canadian Heavy Battery war diary.
**Public Works and Government Services Canada**
Translation of battle report of 119 RIR, 24 June to 14 July 1916.
**Liddell Hart Archive, Kings College, London**
Beauvoir de Lisle, *My narrative of the Great German War*, 1919.
**National Media Museum, Bradford**
Urban Papers.


## PRINTED BOOKS, CD-ROMS AND INTERNET SITES

Ashurst, G. 1987. *My bit. A Lancashire Fusilier at war 1914–18* (Crowood Press, Ramsbury)

Astill, E. 2007. *The Great War diaries of Brigadier Alexander Johnston 1914–1917* (Pen & Sword, Barnsley)

Barton, P. 2005. *The battlefields of the First World War. The unseen panoramas of the Western Front* (Constable, London)

Barton, P. 2006. *The Somme* (Constable, London)

Blumberg, H.E. 1927. *Britain's sea soldiers: a record of the Royal Marines during the war 1914–1919* (Swiss & Co., Devonport)

Brennert, H. 1917. *Bei unserern Helden an der Somme* (Eysler & Co., Berlin)

Brownlow, K. 1979. *The war, the west and the wilderness* (Secker & Warburg, London)

Bull, S. 1998. *World War One British Army* (Brassey's, London)

Bull, S. 2000. *World War One German Army* (Brassey's, London)

Carver, R.B. 1937. *A history of the 10 (Service) Battalion the East Yorkshire Regiment (Hull Commercials)* (A. Brown, London)

Cave, N. 1994. *Beaumont Hamel. Newfoundland Park* (Leo Cooper, London)

Cave, N. 1998. *Gommecourt* (Leo Cooper, London)

Chapman, G.A. 1985. *A passionate prodigality* (Ashford, Buchan & Enright, Leatherhead)

Chappell, M. 1986. *British battle insignia (1): 1914–18* (Osprey, London)

Clarke, D. 2004. *British artillery 1914–19 Field army artillery* (Osprey, London)

Clarke, D. 2005. *British artillery 1914–19 Heavy artillery* (Osprey, London)

Committee of Imperial Defence 1932 and 1938, *History of the Great War based on Official Documents. Military Operations France and Belgium: 1916* (Macmillan, London)

Commonwealth War Graves Commission 2006 'Debt of honour register' at http://www.cwgc.org/debt_of_honour.

Crawford, O.G.S. 1955. *Said and done. The autobiography of an archaeologist* (Weidenfeld & Nicolson, London)

Cron, H. 2002. *Imperial German Army 1914–18. Organisation, structure, orders of battle* (Helion, Solihull)

Cron, H. et al [1935]. *Ruhmeshalle unserer alten Armee* (Verlag für Militärgeschichte und deutsches Schrifttum, Berlin)

De Lisle, B. 1939. *Reminiscences of sport and war* (Eyre & Spottiswoode, London)

Dixon, J. 2000. *Out since 14. The history of the 1/2nd Battalion the Monmouthshire Regiment 1914–19* (Old Bakehouse Publications, Abertillery)

Enticknap, L. 2005. *Moving image technology: from zoetrope to digital* (Wallflower Press, London)

Fabeck, H. von. 1930 *Im orkan der Sommeschlacht* (Wilhelm Kolk, Berlin)

Falls, C. 1922. *The history of the 36th Ulster Division* (McCaw, Stevenson & Orr, Belfast)

Farndale, M. 1986. *History of the Royal Regiment of Artillery. Western Front 1914–18* (Royal Artillery Institution, London)

Frederick, J.B.M. 1984. *Lineage book of British land forces 1660–1978* (Microform Academic Publishers, Wakefield)

Frisch, G. 1931. *Das Reserve-Infanterie-Regiment Nr. 109 im Weltkrieg 1914 bis 1918* (Thiergarten, Karlsruhe)

General Staff, British Army. 1928. *Vocabulary of German Military Terms and Abbreviations* (HMSO, London)

General Staff, British Army. 1973. *German Army Handbook, April 1918* (Arms & Armour Press, London)

General Staff, British Army. 1977. *Handbook of the German Army in War, January 1917* (EP Publishing, London)

General Staff, British Army. 1925. *Machine gun training* (HMSO, London)

Gerster, M. 1920. *Das Württemburgische Reserve-Inf.-Regiment Nr. 119 im Weltkrieg 1914–1918* (Chr. Belsersche Verlagbuchshandlung, Stuttgart)

Giles, J. 1986. *The Somme then and now* (After the Battle, Plaistow)

Gliddon, G. 1990. *When the barrage lifts. A topographical history of the Battle of the Somme 1916* (Alan Sutton, Stroud)

Gliddon, G. 1996. *Legacy of the Somme 1916: the battle in fact, film and fiction* (Sutton Publishing, Stroud)

Gliddon, G. 2006. *Somme 1916. A battlefield companion* (Sutton Publishing, Stroud)

Grain, H.W.W. 1935. *The 16 (Public Schools) Service Battalion (The Duke of Cambridge's Own) Middlesex Regiment and the Great War 1914–18* (FP Lewington, London)

Hammerton, J. 1938. *I was there! The human story of the Great War of 1914–1918* (Waverley Book Company, London)

Hart, P. 2005. *The Somme* (Weidenfeld & Nicolson, London)

Hiley, N. nd. 'Making war: the British news media and government control'. Thesis.

Hogg, I.V. 1998. *Allied artillery of World War One* (Crowood Press, Ramsbury)

Hogg, I.V. and Thurston, L.F. 1972. *British artillery weapons and ammunition 1914–1918* (Ian Allen, London)

Holtz, G. von. 1922. *Das Württemburgische Reserve-Inf.-Regiment Nr. 121 im Weltkrieg 1914–1918* (Chr. Belsersche Verlagbuchshandlung, Stuttgart)

Horsfall, J. and Cave, N. 1996. *Serre* (Leo Cooper, London)

Hurst, S. 2007. *The Public Schools Battalion in the Great War: a history of the 16th Middlesex (Public Schools) Battalion of the Middlesex Regiment (Duke of Cambridge's Own). August 1914 to July 1916* (Pen & Sword, Barnsley)

Intelligence Section, General Staff, American Expeditionary Force. 1989. *Histories of the Two Hundred and Fifty One Divisions of the German Army which participated in the War (1914–1918)* (London Stamp Exchange, London)

*Internet Movie Database* (IMDb) at http://uk.imdb.com/

James, E.A. 1978. *British Regiments 1914–1918* (Samson Books, London)

Johnson, R.M. nd. *29 Divisional artillery war record and honours book 1915–1918* (Naval & Military Press/Royal Artillery Museum, Woolwich)

Jones, E.M. 1915. *The cinematographic book: a complete practical guide to the taking and projecting of cinematograph pictures* (Cassell, London)

Latter, J.C. 1949. *The Lancashire Fusiliers 1914–1918* (Gale & Polden, Aldershot)

Lloyd, M. 2001. *The London Scottish in the Great War* (Leo Cooper, London)

Low, R. 1948. *The history of British film* (George Allen & Unwin Ltd, London)

Lytton, N. 1920. *The press and the General Staff* (Collins, London)

Maddocks, G. 1999. *Montauban* (Leo Cooper, London)

Malins, G.H. 1993. *How I filmed the war* (Battery Press/IWM, Nashville)

McCarthy, C. 1993. *The Somme: the day-by-day Account* (Arms & Armour Press, London)

MacDonald, A. *Pro patria mori. The 56 (1 London) Division at Gommecourt, 1 July 1916* (Exposure Publishing, Liskeard)

Messenger, C. 2003. *World War I in colour* (Nugus/Martin Productions, London)

Middlebrook, M. 1971. *The first day on the Somme* (Penguin Books, London)

Middlebrook, M. and M. 1994. *The Somme Battlefields. A comprehensive guide from Crécy to the Two World Wars* (Penguin, London)

Moser, O. von. 1927. *Die Württemberger im Weltkriege* (Chr. Belser A.G., Stuttgart)

Naval and Military Press. 1998. *Soldiers Died in the Great War 1914–19. A Complete and Searchable Digital Database* (Naval & Military Press, Heathfield)

Naval and Military Press. 2003. *Captured German Trench and Operations Maps from the National Archives* (Naval & Military Press, Heathfield)

Naval and Military Press. 2004. *The Imperial War Museum Trench Map Archive on CD-ROM* (Naval & Military Press, Heathfield)

Pegler, M. and Chappell, M. 1996. *British Tommy 1914–1918* (Osprey, London)

Reed, P. 1997. *Walking the Somme* (Leo Cooper, London)

Reeves, N. 1986. *Official British film propaganda during the First World War* (Croom Helm, London)

Reeves, N. 1999. *The power of film propaganda. Myth or reality?* (Continuum, London)

Robertshaw, A. 2006. *Somme 1 July 1916. Triumph and tragedy* (Osprey, London)

Sassoon, S. 1930. *Memoirs of an infantry officer* (Faber & Faber, London)

Saunders, A. 1999. *Weapons of the trench war 1914–1918* (Sutton Publishing, Stroud)

Saunders, N.J. 2007. *Killing time: archaeology and the First World War* (Sutton Publishing, Stroud)

Sheldon, J. 2005. *The German Army on the Somme 1914–1916* (Pen & Sword, Barnsley)

Sheldon, J. 2006 (1). *The Germans at Beaumont Hamel* (Pen & Sword, Barnsley)

Sheldon, J. 2006 (2). *The Germans at Thiepval* (Pen & Sword, Barnsley)

Smither, R. (ed.). 1993. *The Battle of the Somme and The Battle of the Ancre and the Advance of the Tanks* (Imperial War Museum, London)

Soden, Freiherr von. nd. *Die 26 (Württembergische) Reserve-Division im Weltkrieg 1914–1918, I Teil* (Bergers Literarisches Büro und Verlagsanstalt, Stuttgart)

Stedman, M. 1994. *Manchester Pals 16, 17, 18, 19, 20, 21, 22 & 23 Battalions of the Manchester Regiment. A history of the two Manchester brigades* (Leo Cooper, London)

Stedman, M. 1997 (1). *Fricourt-Mametz* (Leo Cooper, London)

Stedman, M. 1997 (2). *La Boisselle, Ovillers/Contalmaison* (Leo Cooper, London)

Stephens, F.J. and Maddocks, G.J. 1975. *Uniforms and Organisation of the Imperial German Army 1900–1918* (Almark, New Malden)

Stosch, A. 1927. *Somme Nord. I. Teil. Die Brennpunkte der Schlacht im Juli 1916* (Stalling, Oldenburg)

Swinton, E. 1935? *Twenty years after. The battlefields of 1914–18 then and now* (George Newnes, London)

Temple, B.A. 1986. *Identification manual on the .303 British service cartridge No. 1. Ball ammunition* (B.A. Temple, Burbank)

Temple, B.A. 1995. *World War One armaments and the .303 British cartridge* (B.A. Temple, Kilcoy)

Toulmin, V., Popple, S. and Russell, P. 2004. *The lost world of Mitchell & Kenyon* (British Film Institute, London)

Uebe, F. 1923. *Das Oberschlesische Feldart.-Regiment Nr. 57* (Gerhard Stelling, Oldenburg)

Walter, J. 2000. *Allied small arms of World War One* (Crowood Press, Ramsbury)

Westlake, R. 1994. *British Battalions on the Somme* (Leo Cooper, London)

Wooley, C. 1999. *Uniforms and equipment of the Imperial German Army 1900–1918. A study in period photographs* (Schiffer, Atglen, Penn.)

## ARTICLES

Badsey, S.D. 1983. 'Battle of the Somme: British war propaganda', in *Historical Journal of Film, Radio and Television* 3:2, 99–115

Buffetaut, Y. (ed.) 2006. 'Somme 1916: la première bataille mediatise', in *Battailles* 19, Dec. 2006/Jan. 2007

Chappell, M. 1986. '1st Lancashire Fusiliers on the Somme, 1 July 1916', in *Military Illustrated*, June/July 1986

Dutton, P. 2004. '"More vivid than the written word": Ellis Ashmead-Bartlett's film, *With the Dardanelles Expedition* (1915)', in *Historical Journal of Film, Radio and Television* 24:2, 205–22

Grundy, R.B. 1986. 'Q744', in *Stand To! The Journal of the Western Front Association* 17, summer 1986

Haggith, T. 2002. 'Reconstructing the musical arrangement for the Battle of the Somme', in *Film History* 14, 11–24

Hudson, C. 2006. 'Silent suffering', in the *Sunday Times Magazine*, 8 Oct. 2006, 16–24

Reeve, N. 1983. 'Film propaganda and its audience: the example of Britain's official films during the First World War', in *Journal of Contemporary History* 18:3, 463–94

Reeve, N. 1996. 'Cinema, spectatorship and propaganda: Battle of the Somme and its contemporary audience – 1916', in *Historical Journal of Film, Radio and Television* 17:1, 5–28

Rother, R. 1995. '*Bei Unseren Helden an der Somme*' (1917): the creation of a "social event"', in *Historical Journal of Film, Radio and Television* 15:4, 525–42

Smither, R. 2002. 'Watch the picture carefully and see if you can identify anyone', in *Film History* 14, 390–404

## PERIODICALS

*Bioscope*
*Bolton and Bury Catholic Herald*
*Bury Times*
*Bury Visitor*
*Cinema*
*Durham Advertiser*
*Durham Chronicle*
*Gallipoli Gazette*
*Kinematograph and Lantern Weekly*
*Lancashire Fusiliers Annual*
*London Scottish Regimental Gazette*
*Newcastle Journal*
*Screen*
*The Times*

# INDEX

## *Index of Army Units*

**British Army**, 1, 31, 46, 135, 140
Third Army, 16, 20
Fourth Army, 136, 173
New Army, 69, 70, 72, 126
III Corps, 61, 76
VII Corps, 16
VIII Corps, 37, 43, 53, 109
X Corps, 38
XV Corps, 63, 67, 129
4 Division, 44, 102, 103
7 Division, 59, *59*, 66, 67, 74, 76, 107, 109, 113, 116, *123*, 124, 131, 133, 134, *138, 151*, 152
17 Division, 129
18 Division, 68, *69*, 70, 136, 152, 156
29 Division, 25, *26, 27, 30*, 33 , 35, 38, *38*, 49, 50, 51, 52, 53, 77, 98, *98*, 103, 113, 117, 152
34 Division, 147
36 (Ulster) Division, 51, 142
48 Division, 35, 75
56 Division, 16, 20
10 Brigade, 44, 104, 106
11 Brigade, 45
22 Brigade 66, 134
35 Brigade, 133
86 Brigade, 25, *53*, 140
88 Brigade, 25, 26, *26, 30*
91 Brigade, 59, 76
161 Brigade, 16
Army Service Corps, 15
Army Service Corps (TF), 102
Machine Gun Corps, 41
10 Brigade Machine Gun Company, 44, 104, 106
11 Brigade Machine Gun Company, 45
Bedfordshire Regiment, 70, 72, 157
1 Bedfords, 99
7 Bedfords, 70, *71*, 157
Berkshire Regiment, 102
1 Border Regiment, 99
7 East Kent Regiment, *69*
VIII Corps Cavalry Regiment, 142
XV Corps Cyclist Battalion, 107
Devonshire Regiment, 129, 131
8 Devons, 131, 133
9 Devons, 64, 129, 131
29 Divisional Ammunition Column, *34*
53 (Welsh) Divisional Ammunition Column, *34*
Duke of Cornwall's Light Infantry, 161
12 DCLI, *162*
East Lancashire Regiment, 77
1 East Lancs, 77, 78
East Yorkshire Regiment, 23, *24*
Essex Regiment, 152
1 Essex, 152
10 Essex, 152–3
Hampshire Regiment, 26, *26, 28, 30*
King's West African Rifles, 81
Gordon Highlanders, 129, 131, 132
2 Gordon Highlanders, 64, 109, 124
Lancashire Hussars Yeomanry, 142
Lancashire Fusiliers, 57, 82, 84, 85, *85, 97*
1 Lancs Fus., *36*, 53, *54*, 56, *56*, 78, 79, 82, *85*, 86, 94, 100, 102, *105*
2 Lancs Fus., 82, 102
5 Lancs Fus., 82
10 Lancs Fus., 129
37 Lancers (Baluch Horse), 134
London Scottish, 7, 15, 16, 20, *22*
1 London Scottish, 16, 23
Manchester Pioneers, 109
Manchester Regiment, 109, 113
10 Manchesters, 82
20 Manchesters, 134
21 Manchesters, 124, 126, 134, 139
22 Manchesters, 59, 126, 134
24 Manchesters, 74, 109, 113, 137
Middlesex Regiment, 70, 77, *78*, 92, 94, *94*, 135
12 Middlesex, 136
16 Middlesex, 70, 77, 78, 92, 94, *94*
Monmouthshire Regiment, 51–2, 81, 86
Northamptonshire Yeomanry, 56
Queen's Regiment, 76
2 Queen's, 76, 120, *121*, 124, 152
Royal Army Medical Corps, 20, *47*, 76, *85*, 98, 99, 100, 109, *110*, 113
22 Field Ambulance, 109, *110*, 111, *111*, 113, 131